PREFACE

Sociology is the study of society and human social action. It generally concerns itself with the social rules and processes that bind and separate people not only as individuals, but as members of associations, groups, and institutions, and includes the examination of the organization and development of human social life. Sociological research ranges from the analysis of short contacts between anonymous individuals on the street to the study of global social processes. Most sociologists work in one or more specialties or subfields.

The word sociology comes from the suffix "-logy" which means "study of," derived from Greek, and the stem "socio" which is from the Latin word socius, meaning member, friend, or ally, thus referring to people in general. It is a social science involving the study of the social lives of people, groups, and societies, sometimes defined as the study of social interactions. As an academic discipline, sociology is relatively young, having evolved in the early 19th century.

This book elaborately studies all the fields of sociology, their aspects and scopes.

CONTENTS

1

HISTORY OF SOCIOLOGY

INTRODUCTION

Sociology is the study of society and human social action. It generally concerns itself with the social rules and processes that bind and separate people not only as individuals, but as members of associations, groups, and institutions, and includes the examination of the organization and development of human social life. Sociological research ranges from the analysis of short contacts between anonymous individuals on the street to the study of global social processes. Most sociologists work in one or more specialties or subfields (listed below).

The word sociology comes from the suffix "-logy" which means "study of," derived from Greek, and the stem "socio" which is from the Latin word socius, meaning member, friend, or ally, thus referring to people in general. It is a social science involving the study of the social lives of people, groups, and societies, sometimes defined as the study of social interactions. As an academic discipline, sociology is relatively young, having evolved in the early 19th century.

Because sociology is such a broad discipline, it can be difficult to define, even for professional sociologists. One useful way to describe the discipline is as a cluster of sub-fields that examine different dimensions of society.

For example, social stratification studies inequality and class structure; demography studies changes in a population size or type; criminology examines criminal behavior and deviance; political sociology studies government and laws; and the sociology of race and sociology of gender examine society's racial and gender cleavages.

New sociological sub-fields continue to appear—such as network analysis—many of which are cross-disciplanary in nature.

Since the late 1970s, many sociologists have tried to make the discipline useful for non-academic purposes. The results of sociological research aid educators, lawmakers, administrators, developers, and others interested in resolving social problems and formulating public policy, through subdisciplinary areas such as survey research, evaluation research, methodological assessment, and public sociology.

Sociological methods, theories, and concepts compel the sociologist to explore the origins of commonly accepted rules governing human behavior. This specific approach to reality is known as the sociological perspective. Sociology is methodologically diverse using both qualitative and quantitative methods, including case studies, survey research, statistical analysis, and model building among others.

HISTORY OF SOCIOLOGY

Sociology is a relatively new academic discipline among other social sciences including economics, political science, anthropology, history, and psychology. The ideas behind it, however, have a long history and can trace their origins to a mixture of common human knowledge and philosophy.

Auguste Comte

Sociology emerged as a scientific discipline in the early 19th century as an academic response to the challenge of modernity: as the world was becoming smaller and more integrated, people's experience of the world was increasingly atomized and dispersed. Sociologists hoped not only to understand what held social groups together, but also to develop an antidote to social disintegration.

The word sociology was coined by Auguste Comte in 1838 from Latin *Socius* (companion, associate) and Greek *lógos* (speech). Comte hoped to unify all studies of humankind--including history, psychology and economics. His own sociological scheme was typical of the 19th century; he believed all human life had passed through the same distinct historical stages (theology, metaphysics, positive science) and that, if one could grasp this progress, one could prescribe the remedies for social ills. Sociology was to be the 'queen of sciences'.

Herbert Spencer

The first book with the term 'sociology' in its title was **The Study of Sociology** (1874) by the English philosopher Herbert Spencer. In the United States, Lester Frank Ward, described by some as the father of American sociology, published **Dynamic Sociology** in 1883 and the discipline was taught by its own name for the first time at the University of Kansas, Lawrence in 1890 under the course title *Elements of Sociology* (the oldest continuing sociology course in America). The *Department of History and Sociology* at the University of Kansas was established in 1891, and the first full fledged independent university department of sociology was established in 1892 at the University of Chicago by Albion W. Small, who in 1895 founded the American Journal of Sociology. The first European department of sociology was founded in 1895 at the University of Bordeaux by Émile Durkheim, founder of L'Année Sociologique (1896). The first sociology department to be established in the United Kingdom was at the London School of Economics and Political Science (home of the British Journal of Sociology) in 1904. In 1919 a sociology department was established in Germany at the Ludwig Maximilians University of Munich by Max Weber and in 1920 in Poland by Florian Znaniecki.

Karl Marx

International cooperation in sociology began in 1893 when René Worms founded the small Institut International de Sociologie that was eclipsed by the much larger International Sociological Association starting in 1949 (ISA). In 1905 the American Sociological Association, the world's largest association of professional sociologists, was founded.

Other "classical" theorists of sociology from the late 19th and early 20th centuries include Karl Marx, Ferdinand Tönnies, Émile Durkheim, Vilfredo Pareto, and Max Weber. Like Comte, these figures did not consider themselves only "sociologists". Their works addressed religion, education, economics, law, psychology, ethics, philosophy, and theology, and their theories have been applied in a variety of academic diciplines. Their most enduring influence, however, has been on sociology, (with the exception of Marx, who is a central figure in the field of economics as well) and it is in this field that their theories are still considered most applicable.

Lester Ward

One shift in the discipline away from scientific explanation had philosophical roots. Early theorists' approach to sociology, led by Comte, was to treat it in the same manner as natural science, applying the same methods and methodology used in the natural sciences to study social phenomena. The emphasis on empiricism and the scientific method sought to provide an incontestable foundation for any sociological claims or findings, and to distinguish sociology from less empirical fields like philosophy.

This methodological approach, called positivism, became a source of contention between sociologists and other scientists, and eventually a point of divergence within the field itself. Thus, while most sciences evolved from deterministic, Newtonian models to probabilistic models which accept and even incorporate uncertainty, sociology began to cleave into those who believed in a deterministic approach (attributing variation to structure, interactions, or other forces) and those who rejected the very possibility of explanation and prediction.

Max Weber

A second push away from scientific explanation was cultural, even sociological, itself. As early as the 19th century, positivist and naturalist approaches to studying social life were questioned by scientists like Wilhelm Dilthey and Heinrich Rickert, who argued that the natural world differs from the social world due to unique aspects of human society such as meanings, symbols, rules, norms, and values. These elements of society both result in and generate human cultures. This view was further developed by Max Weber, who introduced antipositivism (humanistic sociology).

According to this view, which is closely related to antinaturalism, sociological research must concentrate on humans' cultural values. This has led to some controversy on how one can draw the line between subjective and objective research and has also influenced hermeneutical studies. Similar disputes, especially in the era of the Internet, have led to variations in sociology such as public sociology, which emphasizes the usefulness of sociological expertise to abstracted audiences.

SOCIAL THEORY

Social theory refers to the use of abstract and often complex theoretical frameworks to explain and analyze social patterns and macro social structures in social life, rather than explaining patterns of social life. Social theory always had an uneasy relationship to the more classic academic disciplines; many of its key thinkers never held a university position. While social theory is sometimes considered a branch of sociology, it is inherently interdisciplinary, as it deals with multiple fields including anthropology, economics, theology, history, philosophy, and many others.

First social theories developed almost simultaneously with the birth of the sociology science itself. Auguste Comte, known as 'father of sociology'; also laid the groundwork for one of the first social theories—social evolutionism. In the 19th century three great, classical theories of social and historical change were created: the social evolutionism theory (of which social darwinism is a part of), the social cycle theory and the Marxist historical materialism theory.

Although, the majority of 19th century social theories are now considered obsolete they have spawned new, modern social theories. Modern social theories represent some advanced version of the classical theories, like Multilineal theories of evolution (neoevolutionism, sociobiology, theory of modernisation, theory of post-industrial society) or the general historical sociology and the theory of subjectivity and creation of the society.

Unlike disciplines within the natural sciences -- such as physics or chemistry -- social theorists may be less committed to use the scientific method to vindicate their theories. Instead, they tackle very large-scale social trends and structures using hypotheses that cannot be easily proved, except by historical and psychological interpretation, which is often the basis of criticism from opponents of social theories. Extremely critical theorists, such as deconstructionists or postmodernists, may argue that any systematic type of research or method is inherently flawed. Many times, however, "social theory" is defined without reference to science because the social reality it describes is so overarching as to be unprovable. The social theories of modernity or anarchy might be two examples of this.

However, social theories are a major part of the science of sociology. Objective science-based research can often provide support for explanations given by social theorists. Statistical research grounded in the scientific method, for instance, that finds a severe income disparity between women and men performing the same occupation can complement the underlying premise of the complex social theories of feminism or patriarchy.

In general, and particularly among adherents to pure sociology, social theory has an appeal because it takes the focus away from the individual (which is how most humans look at the world) and focuses it on the society itself and the social forces which control our lives. This sociological insight (or sociological imagination) has through the years appealed to students and others dissatisfied with the status quo because it carries the assumption that societal structures and patterns are either random, arbitrary or controlled by specific powerful groups -- thus implying the possibility of change. This has a particular appeal to champions of the underdog, the dispossessed, and/or those at the bottom of the socioeconomic ladder because it implies that their position in society is undeserved and/or the result of oppression.

The Science and Mathematics of Sociology

Sociologists study society and social behavior by examining the groups and social institutions people form, as well as various social, religious, political, and business organizations. They also study the behaviour of, and social interaction among, groups, trace their origin and growth, and analyze the influence of group activities on individual members. Sociologists are concerned with the characteristics of social groups, organizations, and institutions; the ways individuals are affected by each other and by the groups to which they belong; and the effect of social traits such as sex, age, or race on a person's daily life.

The results of sociological research aid educators, lawmakers, administrators, and others interested in resolving social problems and formulating public policy. Most sociologists work in one or more specialties, such as social organization, social stratification, and social mobility; racial and ethnic relations; education; family; social psychology; urban, rural, political, and comparative sociology; sex roles and relationships; demography; gerontology; criminology; and sociological practice.

Although, sociology emerged in large part from Comte's conviction that sociology eventually would subsume all other areas of scientific inquiry, in the end, sociology did not replace the other sciences. Instead, sociology came to be identified with the other social sciences (psychology, economics, etc.).

Today, sociology studies humankind's organizations, social institutions and their social interactions, largely employing a comparative method. The discipline has concentrated particularly on the organization of complex industrial societies. Recent sociologists, taking cues from anthropologists, have noted the "Western emphasis" of the field. In response, many sociology departments around the world are encouraging multi-cultural and multi-national studies.

Today, sociologists research micro-structures that organize society, such as race or ethnicity, social class, gender roles, and institutions such as the family; social processes that represent deviation from, or the breakdown of, these structures, including crime and divorce; and micro-processes such as interpersonal interactions and the socialization of individuals.

Sociologists often rely on quantitative methods of social research to describe large patterns in social relationships and in order to develop models that can help predict social change. Other branches of sociology believe that qualitative methods—such as focused interviews, group discussions and ethnographic methods—allow for a better understanding of social processes.

Some sociologists argue for a middle ground that sees quantitative and qualitative approaches as complementary. Results from one approach can fill gaps in the other approach. For example, quantitative methods could describe large or general patterns while qualitative approaches could help to understand how individuals understand those patterns.

Social Research Methods

There are several main methods that sociologists use to gather empirical evidence, which include questionnaires, interviews, participant observation, and statistical research.

The problem with all of these approaches is that they are all based on what theoretical position the researcher adopts to explain and understand the society the researcher sees in front of themselves. If one is a functionalist like Émile Durkheim, one is likely to interpret everything in terms of large-scale social structures. A symbolic interactionist is likely to concentrate on the way people understand one another.

A researcher who is a Marxist or a neo-Marxist is likely to interpret everything through the grid of class struggle and economics. Phenomenologists tend to think that there is only the way in which people construct their meanings of reality, and nothing else. One of the real problems is that many sociologists argue that only one theoretical approach is the "right" one, and it is theirs. In practice, sociologists often tend to mix and match different approaches and methods, since each method produces particular types of data.

The Internet is of interest for sociologists in three ways: as a tool for research, for example, in using online questionnaires instead of paper ones, as a discussion platform, and as a research topic. Sociology of the Internet in the last sense includes analysis of online communities (e.g. as found in newsgroups), virtual communities and virtual worlds, organisational change catalysed through new media like the Internet, and societal change at-large in the transformation from industrial to informational society (or to information society).

Sociology and Other Social Sciences

In the early 20th century, sociologists and psychologists who conducted research in industrial societies contributed to the development of anthropology. Anthropologists also conducted research in industrial societies. Today sociology and anthropology are better contrasted according to different theoretical concerns and methods rather than objects of study.

Sociobiology is a relatively new field to branch from both the sociology and biology disciplines. Although the field once rapidly gained acceptance, it has remained highly controversial as it attempts to find ways in which social behavior and structures can be explained by evolutionary and biological processes. Sociobiologists are often criticized by Ashwin N. Ramani for depending too greatly on the effects of genes in defining behavior. Sociobiologists often respond, however, by citing a complex relationship between nature and nurture.

In this regard, sociobiology is closely related to physical anthropology, zoology, evolutionary psychology, human behavioral ecology, and dual inheritance theory. Nonetheless, for most in the discipline, its ideas are unacceptable.

Some sociobiologists, such as Richard Machalek, call for the field of sociology to encompass the study of non-human societies along with human beings.

Sociology has some links with social psychology, but the former is more interested in social structures and the latter in social behaviors. A distinction should be made between these and forensic studies within these disciplines, particularly where anatomy is involved. These latter studies might be better named as Forensic psychology. As shown by the work of Marx and others, economics has influenced sociological theories.

A

Andrew Abbott American sociologist at the University of Chicago

Jane Addams (1860-1935), American social worker and reformer

Theodor Adorno (1903-1969), German cultural sociologist (Frankfurt School)

Jeffrey C. Alexander, American sociologist

Louis Althusser (1918-1990), Algerian-French philosopher and sociologist

Hannah Arendt (1906-1975), German political theorist

Raymond Aron (1905 - 1983) French philosopher and sociologist

Johan Asplund (b. 1937) Swedish sociologist.

B

Gregory Bateson (1904-1980), English/American cybernetican

Jean Baudrillard (b. 1929), French cultural theorist

Zygmunt Bauman (b. 1925), British sociologist

Peter Bearman (b.1956) American sociologist

Ulrich Beck (1944-), German sociologist

Daniel Bell (born 1919) sociologist and professor emeritus at Harvard University.

Walter Benjamin (1892-1940), German cultural sociologist

Joseph Berger, American theoretical sociologist

Peter L. Berger (b. 1929), Austro-American sociologist

Henri Bergson (1859-1941), French philosopher

Herbert Blumer (1900 - 1997), American sociologist

Phillip Bonacich American mathematical sociologist

Scott Boorman (b.1949) American sociologist, Professor of sociology at Yale University

Thomas Bottomore (1920-1992), British sociologist

Pierre Bourdieu (1930-2002), French sociologist

Ronald Breiger American Sociologist

Ernest Burgess (1886-1966), Canadian-born sociologist

Judith Butler (b. 1956), American gender theorist

Carter Butts American mathematical sociologist.

C

Manuel Castells (b. 1942), Spanish sociologist and urban planner

Cornelius Castoriadis (1922-1997), Greek philosopher and political theorist

Kathleen Carley American computational sociologist at Carnegie Mellon University

Nancy Chodorow (b. 1944), American sociologist and gender theorist

Richard Cloward(1926-2001), American sociologist

Ronald L. Cohen, American social psychologist

Stanley Cohen, British sociologist (criminology)

James S. Coleman (1926-1995), American sociologist

Auguste Comte (1798-1857), French founder of sociology

Charles Cooley (1864-1929), American sociologist

Stefan Czarnowski (1879-1937), Polish sociologist.

D

Hamid Dabashi, American-Iranian cultural critic and intellectual historian

Robert Dahl (b.1915), American political scientist

Ralf Dahrendorf (b.1929), German-British sociologist and politician

Mathieu Deflem (b.1962), sociologist

Gilles Deleuze (1925 - 1995), French philosopher

Mukul R. Dwivedi (b. 1984), Indo-American cultural critic and sociologist

Nancy Denton, American sociologist and demographer

Georgi Dimitrov Dimitrov, Bulgarian sociologist

G. William Domhoff, American sociologist

Patrick Doreian, Irish-American mathematical sociologist

W.E.B. DuBois (1868-1963), African-American civil rights leader

Émile Durkheim (1858-1917), French sociologist.

E

Norbert Elias (1897-1990), German sociologist

Friedrich Engels (1820-1895), German socialist philosopher

Kai T. Erikson (1931), American sociologist

Amitai Etzioni (1929), American sociologist.

F

Rick Fantasia, American sociologist

Thomas Fararo (b. 1933), American mathematical sociologist

Paul Fauconnet (1874-1938) French sociologist

Katherine Faust American sociologist and social network methodologist

Scott Feld, American mathematical sociologist

Gary Alan Fine (b. 1950), American sociologist

Fei Xiaotong (1910-2005) Chinese sociologist and anthropologist

Heinz von Foerster (1911-2002), Austrian-American cybernetican

Michel Foucault (1926-1984), French sociologist

Charles Fourier (1772-1837), French proto-sociologist

Andre Gunder Frank (1929-2005), German economic historian and sociologist

Sigmund Freud (1856-1939), Austrian psycho-analyst

Hans Freyer (1887 - 1969) German sociologist and philosopher

Gilberto Freyre (1900-1987), Brazilian sociologist

Erich Fromm (1900-1980), German-American psychologist.

G

Francis Galton (1822-1911), English statistican

Harold Garfinkel (b. 1917), Professor Emeritus in sociology at Harvard University

Felix Guattari (1930 - 1992), French institutional psychotherapist, founder of schizoanalysis and ecosophy

Anthony Giddens (b. 1938), English sociologist

Corrado Gini (1884-1965), Italian statistician

Arnold Gehlen (1904 - 1976), German philosopher and sociologist

Theodor Geiger (1891-1952), German-Danish sociologist

Ernest Gellner(1925 - 1995), philosopher and social anthropologist

David Glass, (1911 - 1978), British sociologist

Max Gluckman (1911-1975), South African/English social anthropologist

John H. Goldthorpe (b. 1935), British sociologist

Leo Goodman (b.1928), American social statistician

Erving Goffman (1922-1982), Canadian interactionistic sociologist

Antonio Gramsci (1891-1937), Italian Marxist

Richard Grathoff (1934), German sociologist and phenomenologist

Mark Granovetter, American sociologist

Andrew M. Greeley, American sociologist, priest, author

Ludwig Gumplovicz (1838-1909), Polish-Austrian sociologist, one of the founders of European sociology

James Gadberry (b. 1958), American Sociologist.

H

Jürgen Habermas (b. 1929), German social theorist

Maurice Halbwachs (1877 - 1945) French philosopher and sociologist

Stuart Hall (b. 1932) British cultural theorist

Donna Haraway (b. 1944) American gender and technology theorist

David Harvey (b.1935) British geographer

Georg F. Hegel (1770-1831), German philosopher

Richard Hoggart (b. 1918), British sociologist (Birmingham School, culture studies)

George C. Homans (1910-1989) American behavioural sociologist

Axel Honneth (b. 1949), German social theorist

Max Horkheimer (1895-1973), German social philosopher (Frankfurt School)

Floyd Hunter (b.1912), American sociologist.

I

Octavio Ianni (1926), Brazilian sociologist

Ibn Khaldun (1332-1406), Arab historian and proto-sociologist

Kancha Ilaiah, (1952) Indian political scientist and social activist.

J

Jane Jacobs (b.1916), US/Canadian writer and activist

Lewis Wade Jones (1910 - 1979), African-American sociologist and educator.

K

Elihu Katz American sociologist

Stephen A. Kent Canadian sociologist

Ibn Khaldun (1332/ah732 - 1406/ah808), North African historian, forerunner of modern historiography, sociology and economics

Karin Knorr Cetina (b.1944) Austrian-American sociologist

Alfred L. Kroeber (1876–1960) American anthropologist

Thomas S. Kuhn (1922-1996), American science theorist

Antonina K³oskowska (1919-2001), Polish sociologist.

L

William Labov (b. 1927) American sociolinguist and dialectologist

Jacques Lacan (1901-1981), French psychoanalyst

Ernesto Laclau, Argentinian sociologist

Bruno Latour (1947) French sociologist of science

Paul F. Lazarsfeld (1901-1976) Austrian-American sociologist

Gustave Le Bon (1841-1931) French social psychologist and sociologist

Henri Lefebvre (1901 - 1991), French Marxist philosopher

Claude Lévi-Strauss (b. 1908), French anthropologist

Lucien Lévy-Bruhl (1857-1939) French philosopher, sociologist and ethnographer

Alfred R. Lindesmith (1905-1991), American sociologist of drug policy

Seymour Martin Lipset (b. 1922), American comparativist sociologist

Thomas Luckmann (b. 1927), German sociologist

Niklas Luhmann (1927-1998), German sociologist (systems theory)

Rosa Luxemburg (1870-1919), German socialist theoretician

Robert Staughton Lynd (1892 - 1970) American sociologist

Jean-François Lyotard (1924-1998), French philosopher.

M

Henry Maine (1822-1888), British jurist and legal historian

Robert Morrison MacIver (1882-1970) Scottish-American sociologist.

Bronislaw Malinowski (1884-1942), Polish anthropologist

Thomas Malthus (1766-1834), English demographer

Richard Machalek (b. 1946) American sociologist and sociobiologist

Michael Mann (b. 1942) British-American sociologist

Karl Mannheim (1893-1947), German-speaking sociologist

Herbert Marcuse (1898-1979), German-American sociologist (Frankfurt School)

Wladyslaw Markiewicz (b. 1920) Polish sociologist

Karl Marx (1818-1883), German political philosopher, social theorist (see Marxism)

Douglas Massey, American sociologist

Humberto Maturana(b. 1928), Chilean biologist and philosopher

John Levi Martin American sociologist

Marcel Mauss (1872-1950) French sociologist

Dale McConkey, American sociologist

Robert McKenzie(1917-1981), Canadian-born Politics professor and psephologist.

George Herbert Mead (1863-1931) American philosopher and social psychologist

Margaret Mead (1901-1978), American cultural anthropologist

Henri Mendras (1927-2003), French sociologist, chronicler of *La fin des paysans*

Robert K. Merton (1910-2003) American sociologist

Robert Michels (1876-1936) German political sociologist

C. Wright Mills (1916-1962) American sociologist

J. Clyde Mitchell (1918-1995) British Social Anthropologist

Brij Mohan (1939--), Indian-American social scientist

James Moody American mathematical sociologist

James D. Montgomery American economist and mathematical sociologist

Charles Murray (b. 1943) American sociologist.

N

Oswald von Nell-Breuning (1890-1991), German Roman Catholic theologian, sociologist and social reformer

Otto Neurath (1882-1945), Austrian sociologist and political economist

Peter Neville (d. 2002) British further education lecturer and sociologist

Ng Chun Hung, Hong Kong Sociologist, specialized in Hong Kong Popular Culture

Robert Nisbet (1913-1996), American sociologist

Helga Nowotny, Austrian sociologist.

O

William F. Ogburn (1886 - 1959), American sociologist

Claus Offe (1940), German sociologist

Lloyd Ohlin, American sociologist

Franz Oppenheimer (1864-1943) German sociologist and political economist

Stanislaw Ossowski (1897-1963), Polish sociologist

Robert Owen (1771 - 1858), Welsh social reformer.

P

Vilfredo Pareto (1848-1923), Italian economist and sociologist

Robert E. Park (1864 - 1944), American sociologist

Vance Packard (1914-1996), American proto-pop-sociologist

Ray Pahl, British sociologist

Talcott Parsons (1902-1979), American functionalist sociologist

Karl Pearson (1857-1936), English statistician

Jean Piaget (1896 - 1980), Swiss developmental psychologist

Adam Possamai, Belgium sociologist of religion

Nicos Poulantzas (1936-1979), Greek political sociologist

Samuel H. Preston, Professor of Demography, University of Pennsylvania

Robert Putnam (b. 1941), American political scientist

Pierre-Joseph Proudhon (1809-1865) French socialist or anarchist philosopher.

Q and R

Alfred Reginald Radcliffe-Brown (1881–1955) British social anthropologist

Aviad Raz (b. 1968) Israeli sociologist and anthropologist

Jürgen Ritsert, German sociologist

George Ritzer (b. 1940), American sociologist

Terje Rød-Larsen (b. 1947) Norwegian diplomat and sociologist

Eugen Rosenstock-Huessy (1888-1973) German-born social philosopher

Walter Garrison Runciman, 3rd Viscount Runciman of Doxford British sociologist.

S

Harvey Sacks (d. 1975), American sociologist in the ethnomethodology tradition

Henri Saint-Simon (1760 - 1825), French philosopher and social thinker

Saskia Sassen, (b. 1949) American sociologist

Peter Saunders, Australian sociologist

Ferdinand de Saussure (1857-1913), Swiss linguist (structuralism)

Helmut Schelsky (1912-1984), German sociologist

Joseph Alois Schumpeter (1883 - 1950), economist

Alfred Schütz (1899-1959), Austrian philosopher and sociologist (phenomenology)

Richard Sennett (b. 1943), American sociologist and public figure

Ali Shariati (1933-1977), Iranian sociologist

Charles E. Silberman, American criminologist

Albion Woodbury Small (1854-1926), American sociologist, founder of Chicago University Dept. of Sociology

Georg Simmel (1858-1918), German sociologist

John Skvoretz, American mathematical sociologist

Adam Smith(1723-1790), Scottish economist and philosopher

Dorothy E. Smith (b. 1926), British-American sociologist and gender theorist

Werner Sombart (1863-1941), German economist and sociologist

Pitirim Sorokin (1889-1968), Russian sociologist

Herbert Spencer (1820-1903), English philosopher

Oswald Spengler (1880-1936), German philosopher

Steven Spitzer, American sociologist

M N Srinivas (1916 - 1999), Indian sociologist

Anselm L. Strauss (1916 - 1996), American sociologist (sociology of medicine, qualitative methods)

William Graham Sumner (1840-1910), American advocate of Social Darwinism

Eilert Sundt (1817-1875), Norwegian sociologist

Edwin Sutherland (1893-1950), American criminologist

Gerald Suttles, American social constructionist

Jan Szczepañski (1913-2004), Polish sociologist.

T

Gabriel Tarde (1843 - 1904), French sociologist and social psychologist

Laurie Taylor (b.1936), English sociologist and broadcaster

W. I. Thomas (1863 - 1947), American social psychologist

Alexis de Tocqueville (1805 - 1859), French essayist and political analyst

Ferdinand Tönnies (1855-1936), German sociologist.

U and V

Francisco Varela (1946-2001), Chilean biologist and philosopher

Thorstein Veblen (1857-1929), American economist and sociologist

Nildo Viana (b.1965), Brazilian sociologist and philosopher

W

Immanuel Wallerstein, (b. 1930), American sociologist and historian

Stanley Wasserman, Professor of Sociology, Psychology, and Statistics at Indiana University.

Duncan Watts, American mathematical sociologist and network theorist

Peter Wagner, German sociologist and social theorist

Lester Frank Ward (1841-1913), important founder of American sociology

Beatrice Webb (1858-1943), British socialist and social theorist

Sidney Webb (1859-1947), British socialist and social theorist

Alfred Weber (1868-1958), German sociologist

Max Weber (1864-1920), German sociologist

John Westergaard (b. 1927), British sociologist

Edward Westermarck (1862-1939), Finnish sociologist and philosopher

Douglas R. White, (b. 1942), American Mathematical Sociologist and Anthropologist.

Harrison White, American Sociologist

William H. Whyte (b. 1917), American sociologist, journalist and peoplewatcher

William Julius Wilson (b. 1935), American sociologist

Christopher Winship, American sociologist

Louis Wirth (1897 - 1952), German-American sociologist

Edmund Wnuk-Lipinski (b. 1944), Polish sociologist

Mary Wollstonecraft (1759-1797), British social reformer

Erik Olin Wright, American sociologist

Y

Yu Xie Professor of sociology and statistics at the University of Michigan

Z

Benjamin Zablocki (1941-), Professor for sociology of religion and social psychology at Rutgers

Henry Zentner (d. 1986), Professor of sociology at the University of Calgary, Canada.

Eviatar Zerubavel, Cognitive Sociologist, Professor of Sociology at Rutgers

Jean Ziegler (b. 1934), professor of sociology at the University of Geneva and the Sorbonne, Paris.

Slavoj Zizek (b. 1949), Slovenian sociologist and philosopher

Florian Znaniecki (1882-1958), Polish and American sociologist

Irving Zola, medical sociologist and disability rights activist

What Sociology is?

You may be asking: "What do you mean by **applied sociology**?" Well, applied sociology is:

"Any use (often client-centered) of the sociological perspective and/or its tools in the understanding of, intervention in, and/or enhancement of human social life."

Let's dissect this definition. Notice that the definition contains both elements of theory and practice.

"Any use" or application suggests knowledge and a distinct approach. The notion of "client-centered" work requires some thought because it really separates basic from applied work. In client-centered work, someone other than the person investigating it presents the problem.

These problems can be "dirty" in that they exist in natural settings that may, in the best of times, be less than perfect for collecting information or using theory. Yet they are of great value largely because they are real and need solutions!

Sociological perspective refers to identifying patterns in human interaction, how and why these patterns exist, the consequences of them, and how to reproduce or change the patterns.

You will learn more about the sociological perspective in the chapters to follow. For now, understand that there are many ways to "look at" a situation. The sociological perspective is a distinct and powerful way to look at human interactions.

"Understanding of, intervention in and/or "enhancement of human social life" mean that applied sociologists work to advance our collective knowledge of social phenomena, solve problems (intervention), or improve social interaction. Often, applied sociologists work on all three dimensions simultaneously.

We will use the term *applied sociology* throughout this book. We wish it were that simple. Modern sociologists use a variety of terms when they talk about actually applying their discipline. Some sociologists who use the discipline for the purpose of diagnosing and measuring intervention call what they are doing "**clinical sociology**."

Others suggest that *sociological practice* is a better term, because it is a term that denotes both clinical and applied. Knowing these different terms for applied sociology should help you when you read other sociological material. For now, let's just stick to "applied sociology."

Here's an example of basic and applied sociology. What happens when organizations change? Much scientific energy has been devoted to determining how organizations work. How big should they be? What should they look like, or how should they be structured?

What kinds of leaders are best? These questions are all solid sociological questions for which basic researchers have toiled to answer. Basic sociologists initiate projects primarily because of their own interest in the topic. Whatever the topic, they primarily seek to build or test **sociological theory**.

Now, let's look at an applied angle on this same problem. Suppose someone decides to change the organization in which you work. This becomes a real-world problem, not only for the person who needs to lead the change, but also for the person who lives and works in the organization. Wouldn't it be nice if the people responsible for these changes had a little basic theory under their managerial belts? If this sounds as if theory and practice, or basic and applied sciences, are linked, you are right! Good practice demands good theory. Whether formally trained or not, a good plumber knows a great deal of physics' theory. And a good manager needs a good deal of organizational theory.

2

SOCIOLOGY OF ART AND THEORIES

INTRODUCTION

Sociology of art is one of the subfields of sociology. It has grown out of aesthetics as its empirical descendant.

It's goal is not to decide what should or should not be called art, but instead describes what has in fact been called art.

Part of this subfield is the analysis how the honorific 'art' is fought over, what eventually gets labelled art and what doesn't.

Sociology of Architecture

From Wikipedia, the free encyclopedia

Jump to: navigation, search

Sociology of architecture is an uncommon term that describes the sociological study of either:

the built environment

the occupation of architect

Construed as the Sociology of the Built Environment

The sociology of architecture deals with the symbolic interaction between the social actions of the organization of space, for example, cities, parks, houses, bridges, monuments, or other units of construction (like towers and doors), including interior space, and thus, also, the sociology of the architectural profession, of the building industry, and of living.

In Germany Gerhard Grohs, Harald Bodenschatz, and Bernhard Schäfers are cited as examples of those who have done work in this field. Christine Hannemann, with her work "Die Platte," supplied a well-received contribution to industrialized housebuilding in the former East Germany.

Also, the architecture critic and theologian Dieter Hoffmann-Axthelm, of Berlin, created an oblique approach to the discipline with the equally provocative, astute, and exaggeratedly utopian work, "Die dritte Stadt."

Construed as the Sociology of the Architect

The literature is scant in this area, and associated with the American researchers Robert Gutman, Herbert Gans, Dana Cuff, Sherry Ahrentzen, and Linda Groat; most of whose work was conducted from 1980 to 2000. Their most active successor is the Australian researcher Garry Stevens.

Sociology of the Body

From Wikipedia, the free encyclopedia

Jump to: navigation, search

Sociology of the body is a recent branch of sociology studying the representations and social uses of the human body in modern societies.

Human Anatomy

From Wikipedia, the free encyclopedia

Human anatomy or anthropotomy is a special field within anatomy. It studies structures and systems of the **human body**, leaving the study of tissues to histology and cells to cytology. The human body, like the bodies of all animals, consists of systems, that consist of organs, that consist of tissues, that consist of cells.

Sociology of Childhood

From Wikipedia, the free encyclopedia

Jump to : navigation, search

History

In the last two or three decades the sociology of childhood has gained increasing attention and triggered numerous empirical studies as well as intensive theoretical disputes, starting in the Scandinavian and the English-speaking countries. Up to this time, sociology had approached children and childhood mainly from a socialization perspective, and the emergence of the new childhood sociological paradigm ran parallel to the feminist critique of sociological traditions. Childhood sociologists attacked the "adultocentric" approach and the "separative view" of sociology towards children. Not surprisingly, then, the key works in the sociology of childhood are quite interdisciplinary, linking history, cultural studies, ethnomethodology, and pedagogy.

Recent Trends

The current Sociology of childhood is organised around two central discussions:

The Child as a Social Actor

This approach derives from youth sociology as well as ethnography. Focussing on everyday life and the ways children orientate themselves in society, it engages with the cultural performances and the social worlds they construct and take part in. Theory and research methodology approach children as active participants and members of society right from the beginning.

Thus, they are neither analyzed as outsiders to society nor as merely 'emergent' members of society. Therefore, the sociology of childhood distinguishes itself from the established concepts of socialization research and developmental psychology of the last decades.

The Generational Order

The second approach centres on socio-structural and socio-theoretical questions concerning social equality and social order in a society, which categorizes their members by age and segregates them in many respects (rights, deeds, economical participation, ascribed needs etc.). These issues can be summarized under the overall concept of the "generational order".

Thus, the categorization of societal members by age is far from being an innocent representation of natural distinctions, but rather a social construction of such a "natural truth". It is, therefore, a relevant component of social order and deeply connected to other dimensions of social inequality. Social and economic changes and socio-political interventions thus become central topics in childhood sociology. The analysis of these issues has increased awareness of the generational inequality of societies.

Current Tasks

Questions about socialization practices and institutions remain central in childhood research. But, they are being dealt with in a new, more sociological way. To analyze socialization processes means, therefore, to reconstruct the historically and culturally varying conceptions, processes and institutions of disciplining and civilisation of the offspring. In addition, the strategies of habitus formation and the practices of status (re-)production are considered. The sociology of social inequality and the sociology of the family and private life are, therefore, important fields for childhood sociologists. Childrens' own action, their resistance, cooperation, and collective action among peers has to be taken into account. Meanwhile widespread anthropological assumptions concerning a universal human nature , based on a view of individual and society as opposed to each other, should be omitted from the conceptual repertoire of sociological childhood research. They are the legacy of the older socialization approach and they legitimate some forms of childhood and education practices as indispensable and even as a "natural" requirement of society, while devaluing others. In this way they generally legitimate western middle class childhood and mask social inequality and the interests of social order.

Collective Behavior

From Wikipedia, the free encyclopedia

Jump to: navigation, search.

Collective behavior is a specialized term in sociology. The term was first used by Robert E. Park, and employed definitively by Herbert Blumer, to refer to social processes and events which do not reflect existing social structure (laws, conventions, and institutions), but which emerge in a "spontaneous" way. Some examples of collective behavior include religious revivals, a panic in a burning theatre, an outbreak of swastika painting, a change in popular preferences in toothpaste, the Russian Revolution, and a sudden widespread interest in body piercing. Since such events occur when social prescriptions are not clear, they exemplify neither conformity nor deviance.

The claim that this set of seemingly diverse episodes constitutes a single field of inquiry is a theoretical assertion which not all sociologists will agree with. However, its usage by Blumer and Smelser shows that the formulation must satisfy some sociological minds.

Four Forms of Collective Behavior

Most of the examples of collective behavior mentioned above are instances of *crowd behavior*. The classic treatment of crowds is Gustave LeBon, *The Crowd: A Study of the Popular Mind* (1896), in which LeBon, a frightened aristocrat, interpreted the crowds of the French Revolution as irrational reversions to animal emotion, and infers from this that such reversion is characteristic of crowds in general. Freud expressed a similar view in his *Group Psychology and the Analysis of the Ego* (1922).

At the University of Chicago, Robert Park and Herbert Blumer saw crowds as emotional, but as capable of any emotion, not only the negative ones of anger and fear.

All of these writers acknowledge that there are crowds in which the participants are not assembled in one place. Turner and Killian refer to such episodes as *diffuse crowds,* examples being stock market booms, panics about sexual perils, and "Red scares."

Some psychologists have suggested that there are three fundamental human emotions, fear, joy, and anger, and Smelser and others have proposed three corresponding forms of the crowd: the panic, in which fear is the dominant emotion, the craze, which is an expression of joy, and the hostile outburst, which is characterized by anger.

Each of the three emotions can characterize either a *compact* or a *diffuse* crowd, so that there are six types of crowds in this scheme.

Park distinguished the **crowd**, which expresses a *common emotion* from a **public,** in which a *single issue* is discussed. A public exists for every issue being discussed at a particular time, so that there are as many publics as there are issues, each public coming into being when its issue is first raised and going out of being when the issue is resolved.

To the crowd and the public, Blumer added a third form of collective behavior, the **mass.** It differs from both the crowd and the public in that it is not defined by a form of interaction but by presentation from the mass media to an audience. The invention of printing made masses possible, and they have become more prominent still with the invention of each of the other mass media.

The messages from the mass media is an attempt to persuade the mass to choose something which is offered, such as some brand of refrigerator.

The mass acts not by the expression of a common emotion as does the crowd, nor by discussion as does the public, but by the simultaneous and independent action of the participants. Their aggregated choices can have powerful effects on society, as when a popular TV show leads many people to use the bathroom at the same time, so that bond issues have to be floated to increase sewage disposal facilities.

Contrary to Blumer, evidence confirms the common sense view that consumers do not act independently of one another but frequently discuss their choices. For this reason, Turner and Killian suggest that the mass is best thought of as what Max Weber calls an "ideal type" -- not an accurate description of empirical cases, but a concept which is useful in interpreting particular events insofar as they approximate it. Actually, most or all terms in the field refer to ideal types; there are many mixed cases.

We change intellectual gears when we confront Blumer's final form of collective behavior, the **social movement**. Some examples include the French Revolutions, the movement for the adoption of a World Calendar, and Alcoholics Anonymous.

Social movemements typically have a structure and persistrence which distinguishes them from the other three forms of collective behavior, and for this reason they are often considered to be a separate topic.

There have never been many specialists in collective behavior, and these few have typically been students of Park and Blumer at Chicago, or, more recently, of Blumer and Smelser at Berkeley. Thus, collective behavior has been a school of thought as well as a subfield of sociology.

The study of collective behavior spun its wheels for many years, until Neil Smelser's *Theory of Collectiove Behavior* (1962) and social disturbances in the U. S. and elsewhere in the late 60's and early 70's prompted a renewal of interest in the field. Out of this interest has come a number of empirical challenges to the armchair sociology of earlier students of collective behavior.

Richard Berk uses game theory to suggest that even a panic in a burning theater can reflect rational calculation. If members of the audience decide that it is more rational to run to the exits than to walk, the result may look like an animal-like stampede without in fact being irrational.

In a series of empirical studies of assemblies of people, Clark McPhail (*The Myth of the Madding Crowd*) argues that such assemblies vary along a number of dimensions, and that traditional stereotypes of emotionality and unanimity often do not describe what happens.

Conflict Theory

From Wikipedia, the free encyclopedia

Jump to: navigation, search

In sociology, **conflict theory** states that the society or organization functions so that each individual participant and its groups struggle to maximize their benefits, which inevitably contributes to social change such as changes in politics and revolutions. The theory is mostly applied to explain conflict between social classes in ideologies such as capitalism. The theory attempts to refute functionalism, which considers that societies and organization function so that each individual and group plays a specific role, like organs in the body. There are radical basic assumptions (society is eternally in conflict, which might explain social change), or moderate ones (custom and conflict are always mixed). The moderate version allows for functionalism to operate as an equally acceptable theory since it would accept that even negative social institutions play a part in society's self-perpetuation.

The essence of conflict theory is best epitomized by the classic 'pyramid structure' in which an elite dictates terms to the larger masses. All major institutions, laws, and traditions in the society are designed to support those who have traditionally been in power, or the groups that are perceived to be superior in the society according to this theory. This can also be expanded to include any society's 'morality' and by extension their definition of deviance. Anything that challenges the control of the elite will likely be considered 'deviant' or 'morally reprehensible.' The theory can be applied on both the macro level (like the US government or Soviet Russia, historically) or the micro level (a church organization or school club). In summary, conflict theory seeks to catalogue the ways in which those in power seek to stay in power.

In understanding conflict theory, competition plays a key part.

The following are four primary assumptions of modern conflict theory:

1. Competition. Competition over scarce resources (money, leisure, sexual partners, and so on) is at the heart of all social relationships. Competition rather than consensus is characteristic of human relationships.
2. Structural inequality. Inequalities in power and reward are built into all social structures. Individuals and groups that benefit from any particular structure strive to see it maintained.
3. Revolution. Change occurs as a result of conflict between competing interests rather than through adaptation. It is often abrupt and revolutionary rather than evolutionary.
4. War. Even war is a unifier of the societies involved, as well as war may set an end to whole societies.

Conflict theory was elaborated e. g. in the United Kingdom by Max Gluckman and John Rex, in the United States by Lewis A. Coser and Randall Collins, and in Germany by Ralf Dahrendorf, all of them being less or more influenced by Karl Marx, Ludwig Gumplovicz, Vilfredo Pareto, Georg Simmel, and other founding fathers of European sociology.

Social Conflict Theory

From Wikipedia, the free encyclopedia

(Redirected from Social-conflict theory)

Jump to: navigation, search

Social conflict theory is a Marxist-based social theory which argues that individuals and groups (social classes) within society have differing amounts of material and non-material resources (the wealthy vs. the poor) and that the more powerful groups use their power in order to exploit groups with less power.

The two methods by which this exploitation is done are through brute force and economics. Earlier social conflict theorists argue that money is the mechanism which creates social disorder. The theory further states that society is created from ongoing social conflict between various groups.

A homeless American.

Oil Tycoon: John D. Rockefeller

"Consider paying rent towards housing. The conflict theorist argues that this relationship is unequal and favors the owners. Renters may pay rent for 50 years and still gain absolutely no right or economic interest with the property. It is this type of relationship which the conflict theorist will use to show that social relationships are about power and exploitation."

Padgitt continues, "Marx argued that through a dialectic process, social evolution was directed by the result of class conflict. Marxism argues that human history is all about this conflict, a result of the strong-rich exploiting the poor-weak. From such a perspective, money is made through the exploitation of the worker. It is argued thus, that in order for a factory owner to make money, he must pay his workers less than they deserve."

Critical Theory

From Wikipedia, the free encyclopedia

In the humanities and social sciences, **critical theory** has two quite different meanings with different origins and histories, one originating in social theory and the other in literary criticism. Though until recently these two meanings had little to do with each other, since the 1970s there has been some overlap between these disciplines. This has led to "critical theory" becoming an umbrella term for an array of theories within the academic world of the United Kingdom and North America. This article focuses primarily on the differences and similarities between them.

Critical Theory (Social Theory)

The first meaning of the term *critical theory* was that defined by Max Horkheimer of the Frankfurt School of social science in his 1937 essay *Traditional and Critical Theory*: Critical theory is social theory oriented toward critiquing and changing society as a whole, in contrast to traditional theory oriented only to understanding or explaining it. Horkheimer wanted to distinguish critical theory as a radical, emancipatory form of Marxian theory both from the model of science put forward by logical positivism and from what he and his colleagues perceived as the covert positivism and authoritarianism of orthodox Marxism and Communism. It is also central to this notion that critical social theory be directed at the totality of society in its historical specificity, i.e. in the way it had come to be configured at a specific point in time, and that it integrates all of the major social science theories that will help grasp the major dimensions of society, including especially economics, sociology, history, political science, anthropology, and psychology. Although this conception of critical theory originated with the Frankfurt School, it also prevails among some other recent social scientists, such as Pierre Bourdieu, Louis Althusser and arguably Michel Foucault and certain feminist theorists and social scientists.

This version of "critical" theory derives from Kant's (18th-century) and Marx's (19th century) use of the term "critique", as in Kant's *Critique of Pure Reason* and Marx's notion of his work *Das Kapital* (*Capital*) as "the critique of political economy".

For Kant's transcendental idealism, "critique" means examining and establishing the limits of the validity of a faculty, type, or body of knowledge, especially through taking stock of the limitations imposed by the fundamental, irreducible concepts in use in that knowledge. His notion also already associated critique with the disestablishment of false, unprovable, or dogmatic philosophical, social, and political beliefs since for him the critique of reason involved the critique of dogmatic theological and metaphysical ideas and was intertwined with the enhancement of ethical autonomy and the Enlightenment critique of superstition and irrational authority. Marx explicitly developed this notion into the critique of ideology and linked it with the practice of social revolution, as in his famous 11th Thesis on Feuerbach, "Philosophers have only interpreted the world in certain ways; the point is to change it".

This meaning of "critical theory" originated entirely within the social sciences, and there are works of critical social theory and critical social science that pay no attention and show no awareness of the literary/humanities version of critical theory.

CRITICAL THEORY (LITERARY CRITICISM)

The second meaning of *critical theory* is that of theory used in literary criticism - hence "critical theory" -- and in the analysis and understanding of literature and is discussed in greater detail under literary theory.

It is not necessarily oriented toward radical social change or even toward the analysis of society but is focused primarily on the analysis of texts and textlike phenomena. It originated among literary scholars and in the discipline of literature in the 1960s and 1970s and really came into broad use only since the 1980s, especially as theory used in literary studies became increasingly influenced by Continental philosophy and social theory and thereby became more "theoretical".

This version of "critical" theory derives from the notion of literary criticism as establishing and enhancing the proper aesthetic understanding and evaluation of literature, as articulated, for example, in Joseph Addison's notion of a critic as one who helps understand and interpret literary works: "A true critic ought to dwell rather upon excellencies than imperfections, to discover the concealed beauties of a writer, and communicate to the world such things as are worth their observation.". This notion of criticism ultimately goes back to Aristotle's *Poetics* as a theory of literature.

This meaning of "critical theory" originated entirely within the humanities. However, there are works of literary critical theory that show no awareness of the sociological version of critical theory.

RELATIONSHIP BETWEEN THE TWO VERSIONS

These two meanings of critical theory derive from two different intellectual traditions associated with the meaning of criticism and critique, both of which derive ultimately from the Greek word *kritikos* meaning judgment or discernment and in their present forms go back to the 18th century. While they can be considered completely independent intellectual pursuits, increasingly scholars are interested in the areas of critique where the two overlap.

To use an epistemological distinction introduced by Jürgen Habermas in 1968 in his *Erkenntnis und Interesse* (*Knowledge and Human Interests*), critical theory in literary studies is ultimately a form of hermeneutics, i.e. knowledge via interpretation to understand the meaning of human texts and symbolic expressions, while critical social theory is, in contrast, a form of self-reflective knowledge involving both understanding and theoretical explanation to reduce entrapment in systems of domination or dependence, obeying the emancipatory interest in expanding the scope of autonomy and reducing the scope of domination.

From this perspective, much literary critical theory, since it is focused on interpretation and explanation rather than on social transformation, would be regarded as positivistic or traditional rather than critical theory in the Kantian or Marxian sense. Critical theory in literature and the humanities in general does not necessarily involve a normative dimension, whereas critical social theory does, either through criticizing society from some general theory of values, norms, or oughts, or through criticizing it in terms of its own espoused values.

Overlap Between the Two Versions of Critical Theory

Nevertheless, a certain amount of overlap has come about, initiated both from the critical social theory and the literary-critical theory sides. It was distinctive of the Frankfurt School's version of critical theory from the beginning, especially in the work of Max Horkheimer, Theodor Adorno, Walter Benjamin, Herbert Marcuse, and Leo Lowenthal, because of their focus on the role of false consciousness and ideology in the perpetuation of capitalism, to analyze works of culture, including literature, music, art, both "high culture" and "popular culture" or "mass culture." Thus it was to some extent a theory of literature and a method of literary criticism (as in Walter Benjamin's interpretation of Baudelaire and Kafka, Leo Lowenthal's interpretations of Shakespeare, Ibsen, etc., Adorno's interpretations of Kafka, Valery, Balzac, Beckett, etc.) and (see below) in the 1960s started to influence the literary sort of critical theory.

WITHIN SOCIAL THEORY

In the late 1960s Juergen Habermas of the Frankfurt School, redefined critical theory in a way that freed it from a direct tie to Marxism or the prior work of the Frankfurt School. In Habermas's epistemology, critical knowledge was conceptualized as knowledge that enabled human beings to emancipate themselves from forms of domination through self-reflection and took psychoanalysis as the paradigm of critical knowledge. This expanded considerably the scope of what counted as critical theory within the social sciences, which would include such approaches as world systems theory, feminist theory, postcolonial theory, critical race theory, queer theory, social ecology, the theory of communicative action (Habermas), structuration theory, and neo-Marxian theory.

WITHIN LITERARY THEORY

From the literary side, starting in the 1960s literary scholars, reacting especially against the New Criticism of the previous decades, which tried to analyze literary texts purely internally, began to incorporate into their analyses and interpretations of literary works initially semiotic, linguistic, and interpretive theory, then structuralism, Lacanian psychoanalysis, post-structuralism, and deconstruction as well as Continental philosophy, especially phenomenology and hermeneutics, and critical social theory and various other forms of neo-Marxian theory. Thus literary criticism became highly theoretical and some of those practicing it began referring to the theoretical dimension of their work as "critical theory", i.e. philosophically inspired theory of literary criticism. And thus incidentally critical theory in the sociological sense also became, especially among literary scholars of left-wing sympathies, one of a number of influences upon and streams within critical theory in the literary sense.

Furthermore, along with the expansion of the mass media and mass/popular culture in the 1960s and 1970s and the blending of social and cultural criticism and literary criticism, the methods of both kinds of critical theory sometimes intertwined in the analysis of phenomena of popular culture, as in the emerging field of cultural studies, in which concepts deriving from Marxian theory, post-structuralism, semiology, psychoanalysis and feminist theory would be found in the same interpretive work. Both strands were often present in the various modalities of postmodern theory.

Collective Behavior

From Wikipedia, the free encyclopedia

Jump to: navigation, search

Collective behavior is a specialized term in sociology. The term was first used by Robert E. Park, and employed definitively by Herbert Blumer, to refer to social processes and events which do not reflect existing social structure (laws, conventions, and institutions), but which emerge in a "spontaneous" way.

Some examples of collective behavior include religious revivals, a panic in a burning theatre, an outbreak of swastika painting, a change in popular preferences in toothpaste, the Russian Revolution, and a sudden widespread interest in body piercing. Since such events occur when social prescriptions are not clear, they exemplify neither conformity nor deviance.

The claim that this set of seemingly diverse episodes constitutes a single field of inquiry is a theoretical assertion which not all sociologists will agree with. However, its usage by Blumer and Smelser shows that the formulation must satisfy some sociological minds.

Four Forms of Collective Behavior

Most of the examples of collective behavior mentioned above are instances of *crowd behavior*. The classic treatment of crowds is Gustave LeBon, *The Crowd: A Study of the Popular Mind* (1896), in which LeBon, a frightened aristocrat, interpreted the crowds of the French Revolution as irrational reversions to animal emotion, and infers from this that such reversion is characteristic of crowds in general. Freud expressed a similar view in his *Group Psychology and the Analysis of the Ego* (1922).

At the University of Chicago, Robert Park and Herbert Blumer saw crowds as emotional, but as capable of any emotion, not only the negative ones of anger and fear.

All of these writers acknowledge that there are crowds in which the participants are not assembled in one place. Turner and Killian refer to such episodes as *diffuse crowds,* examples being stock market booms, panics about sexual perils, and "Red scares."

Some psychologists have suggested that there are three fundamental human emotions, fear, joy, and anger, and Smelser and others have proposed three corresponding forms of the crowd: the panic, in which fear is the dominant emotion, the craze, which is an expression of joy, and the hostile outburst, which is characterized by anger.

Each of the three emotions can characterize either a *compact* or a *diffuse* crowd, so that there are six types of crowds in this scheme.

Park distinguished the **crowd**, which expresses a *common emotion* from a **public,** in which a *single issue* is discussed. A public exists for every issue being discussed at a particular time, so that there are as many publics as there are issues, each public coming into being when its issue is first raised and going out of being when the issue is resolved.

To the crowd and the public, Blumer added a third form of collective behavior, the **mass.** It differs from both the crowd and the public in that it is not defined by a form of interaction but by presentation from the mass media to an audience. The invention of printing made masses possible, and they have become more prominent still with the invention of each of the other mass media.

The messages from the mass media is an attempt to persuade the mass to choose something which is offered, such as some brand of refrigerator. The mass acts not by the expression of a common emotion as does the crowd, nor by discussion as does the public, but by the simultaneous and independent action of the participants. Their aggregated choices can have powerful effects on society, as when a popular TV show leads many people to use the bathroom at the same time, so that bond issues have to be floated to increase sewage disposal facilities.

Contrary to Blumer, evidence confirms the common sense view that consumers do not act independently of one another but frequently discuss their choices. For this reason, Turner and Killian suggest that the mass is best thought of as what Max Weber calls an "ideal type" -- not an accurate description of empirical cases, but a concept which is useful in interpreting particular events insofar as they approximate it. Actually, most or all terms in the field refer to ideal types; there are many mixed cases.

We change intellectual gears when we confront Blumer's final form of collective behavior, the **social movement**. Some examples include the French Revolutions, the movement for the adoption of a World Calendar, and Alcoholics Anonymous.

Social movemements typically have a structure and persistrence which distinguishes them from the other three forms of collective behavior, and for this reason they are often considered to be a separate topic.

There have never been many specialists in collective behavior, and these few have typically been students of Park and Blumer at Chicago, or, more recently, of Blumer and Smelser at Berkeley.

Thus, collective behavior has been a school of thought as well as a subfield of sociology.

The study of collective behavior spun its wheels for many years, until Neil Smelser's *Theory of Collectiove Behavior* (1962) and social disturbances in the U. S. and elsewhere in the late 60's and early 70's prompted a renewal of interest in the field.

Out of this interest has come a number of empirical challenges to the armchair sociology of earlier students of collective behavior.

Richard Berk uses game theory to suggest that even a panic in a burning theater can reflect rational calculation.

If members of the audience decide that it is more rational to run to the exits than to walk, the result may look like an animal-like stampede without in fact being irrational.

In a series of empirical studies of assemblies of people, Clark McPhail (*The Myth of the Madding Crowd*) argues that such assemblies vary along a number of dimensions, and that traditional stereotypes of emotionality and unanimity often do not describe what happens.

Sociology of Architecture

From Wikipedia, the free encyclopedia

Jump to: navigation, search

Sociology of architecture is an uncommon term that describes the sociological study of either:

the built environment

the occupation of architect

Construed as the Sociology of the Built Environment

The sociology of architecture deals with the symbolic interaction between the social actions of the organization of space, for example, cities, parks, houses, bridges, monuments, or other units of construction (like towers and doors), including interior space, and thus, also, the sociology of the architectural profession, of the building industry, and of living.

In Germany Gerhard Grohs, Harald Bodenschatz, and Bernhard Schäfers are cited as examples of those who have done work in this field. Christine Hannemann, with her work "Die Platte," supplied a well-received contribution to industrialized housebuilding in the former East Germany. Also, the architecture critic and theologian Dieter Hoffmann-Axthelm, of Berlin, created an oblique approach to the discipline with the equally provocative, astute, and exaggeratedly utopian work, "Die dritte Stadt."

Construed as the Sociology of the Architect

The literature is scant in this area, and associated with the American researchers Robert Gutman, Herbert Gans, Dana Cuff, Sherry Ahrentzen, and Linda Groat; most of whose work was conducted from 1980 to 2000. Their most active successor is the Australian researcher Garry Stevens.

LANGUAGE AND CONSTRUCTION

The two points at which there is the greatest overlap or mutual impingement of the two versions of critical theory are in their interrelated foci on language, symbolism, and communication and in their focus on construction.

LANGUAGE AND COMMUNICATION

From the 1960s and 1970s onward, language, symbolism, text, and meaning became foundational to theory in the humanities and social sciences, through the short-term and long-term influences of Ludwig Wittgenstein, Ferdinand de Saussure, George Herbert Mead, Noam Chomsky, Hans-Georg Gadamer, Roland Barthes, Jacques Derrida and other thinkers in the traditions of linguistic and analytic philosophy, structural linguistics, symbolic interactionism, hermeneutics, semiology, linguistically oriented psychoanalysis (Lacan, Lorenzer), deconstruction. When, in the 1970s and 1980s, Habermas also redefined critical social theory as a theory of communication, i.e. communicative competence and communicative rationality on the one hand, distorted communication on the other, the two versions of critical theory began to overlap or intertwine to a much greater degree than before.

Construction

Both versions of critical theory have focused on the processes of synthesis, production, or construction by which the phenomena and objects of human communication, culture, and consciousness come about.

Whether it is through the transformational rules by which the deep structure of language becomes its surface structure (Chomsky), the universal pragmatic principles through which mutual understanding is generated (Habermas), the semiotic rules by which objects of daily usage or of fashion obtain their meanings (Barthes), the psychological processes by which the phenomena of everyday consciousness are generated (psychoanalytic thinkers), the *episteme* that underlies our cognitive formations (Foucault), and so on, there is a common interest in the processes (often of a linguistic or symbolic kind) that give rise to observable phenomena. Here there is significant mutual influence among aspects of the different versions of critical theory. Ultimately this emphasis on production and construction goes back to the revolution wrought by Kant in philosophy, namely his focus in the *Critique of Pure Reason* on synthesis according to rules as the fundamental activity of the mind that creates the order of our experience.

COMPARATIVE SOCIOLOGY

From Wikipedia, the free encyclopedia

Jump to: navigation, search

Comparative sociology generally refers to sociological analysis that involves comparison of social processes between nation-states, or across different types of society (for example capitalist and socialist).

There are two main approaches to comparative sociology: some seek similarity across different countries and cultures whereas others seek variance. For example, structural Marxists have attempted to use comparative methods to discover the general processes that underlie apparently different social orderings in different societies. The danger of this approach is that the different social contexts are overlooked in the search for supposed universal structures. One sociologist who employed comparative methods to understand variance was Max Weber, whose studies attempted to show how differences between cultures explained the different social orderings that had emerged (see for example The Protestant Ethic and the Spirit of Capitalism and Sociology of Religion).

There is some debate within sociology regarding whether the label of 'comparative' is suitable. Emile Durkheim argued in The Rules of Sociological Method (1895) that all sociological research was in fact comparative since social phenomenon are always held to be typical, representative or unique, all of which imply some sort of comparison. In this sense, all sociological analysis is comparative and it has been suggested that what is normally referred to as comparative research, may be more appropriately called cross-national research.

COMPUTATIONAL SOCIOLOGY

From Wikipedia, the free encyclopedia

Jump to: navigation, search

Computational sociology is a recently developed branch of sociology that uses computation to analyze social phenomena. The basic premise of computational sociology is to take advantage of computer simulation in the construction of social theories. It involves the understanding of social agents, the interaction among these agents, and the effect of these interactions on the social aggregate. Although the subject matter and methodologies in social science differ from those in natural science or computer science, several of the approaches used in contemporary social simulation originated from fields such as physics and artificial intelligence.

In relevant literature, computational sociology is often related to the study of social complexity. Social complexity concepts such as complex systems, non-linear interconnection among macro and micro process, and emergence, have entered the vocabulary of computational sociology. A practical and well-known example is the construction of a computational model in the form of an "artificial society," by which researchers can analyze the structure of a social system.

CRIMINOLOGY

Criminology is the scientific study of crime as an individual and social phenomenon. Criminological research areas in particular comprise the incidence and forms of crime as well as its causes and consequences. They also include social and governmental regulations and reactions to crime. Criminology is an interdisciplinary field in the behavioural sciences, drawing especially on the research of sociologists and psychologists, as well as on writings in law.

In 1885, Italian law professor Raffaele Garofalo coined the term "criminology" (in Italian, *criminologia*). The French anthropologist Paul Topinard used it for the first time in French (*criminologie*) in 1887.

Schools of Thought

Over time, several schools of thought have developed and are listed in the infobox. The main thematic distinction has been between the: Classical School associated with Cesare Beccaria, Jeremy Bentham, among others, who have argued that:

People have free will to choose how to act.

Deterrence is based upon the utilitarian ontological notion of the human being a 'hedonist' who seeks pleasure and avoids pain, and a 'rational calculator' weighing up the costs and benefits of the consequences of each action. Thus, it ignores the possibility of irrationality and unconscious drives as motivational factors.

Punishment (of sufficient severity) can deter people from crime, as the costs (penalties) outweigh benefits. and the Positivist School which presumes that criminal behaviour is caused by biological, psychological, or social determining factors that predispose some people towards crime. Cesare

Lombroso, an Italian prison doctor working in the late 19th century and sometimes regarded as the "father" of criminology, was one of the largest contributors to biological positivism, which alleged that physiological traits such as the measurements of one's cheek bones or hairline, or a cleft palate, considered to be throwbacks to Neanderthal man, were indicative of "atavistic" criminal tendencies.

This approach, influenced by the earlier theory of phrenology and by Charles Darwin and his theory of evolution, has been superseded, but more modern research examines genetic characteristics and the chemistry of nutrition to determine whether there is an effect on violent behaviour (see Natural Justice).

Hans Eysenck (1964, 1977), a British psychologist, claimed that psychological factors such as Extraversion and Neuroticism made a person more likely to commit criminal acts.

He also includes a Psychoticism dimension that includes traits similar to the psychopathic profile, developed by Cleckley and later Hare. He also based his model on early parental socialization of the child; his approach bridges the gap between biological explanations and environmental or social learning based approaches, (see e.g. social psychologists B. F. Skinner (1938), Albert Bandura (1973), and the topic of "nature vs. nurture".)

Sociological positivism (the father of which is considered to be Emile Durkheim) postulates that societal factors such as poverty, membership of subcultures, or low levels of education can predispose people to crime.

THEORIES OF CRIME

There are many theories, including:

Strain Theory

Based on the work of American sociologist Robert Merton, this theory suggests that mainstream culture, especially in the United States, is saturated with dreams of opportunity, freedom and prosperity; as Merton put it, the *American Dream*. Most people buy into this dream and it becomes a powerful cultural and psychological motivation. Merton also used the term *anomie*, but it meant something slightly different for him than it did for Durkheim; he saw the term as meaning a dichotomy between what society expected of its citizens, and what those citizens could actually achieve.

Therefore, if the social structure of opportunities is unequal and prevents the majority from realising the dream, some of them will turn to illegitimate means (crime) in order to realise it. Others will retreat or drop out into deviant subcultures (gang members, "hobos": urban homeless drunks and drug abusers).

Symbolic Interactionism

Drawing on the phenomenology of Edmund Husserl and George Herbert Mead, subcultural theory and conflict theory, this school of thought focused on the relationship between the powerful state, media and conservative ruling elite on the one hand, and the less powerful groups on the other. The powerful groups had the ability to become the 'significant other' in the less powerful groups' processes of generating meaning. The former could to some extent impose their meanings on the latter, and therefore they were able to 'label' minor delinquent youngsters as criminal.

These youngsters would often take on board the label, indulge in crime more readily and become actors in the 'self-fulfilling prophecy' of the powerful groups. Later developments in this set of theories were by Howard Becker and Edwin Lemert, in the mid 20th century; also by Stanley Cohen who developed the concept of "moral panic" (describing societal reaction to spectacular, alarming social phenomena such as post-World War Two youth cultures (e.g. the *Mods and Rockers* in the UK in 1964), AIDS and football hooliganism.

Control Theories

Another approach is made by the so called "control theories". Instead of looking for factors that make people become criminal, those theories try to explain why people do NOT become criminal. T. Hirschi (1969: Causes of Delinquency) identified four main characteristics: *"attachment to others", "belief in moral validity of rules", "commitment to achievement" and "involvement in conventional activities"*. The more a person features those characteristics, the less are the chances that he or she becomes deviant (or criminal). If—on the other hand—those factors are not present in a person, it is more likely that he or she might become criminal. Hirschi followed up on his own theory with the *theory of low self-control.* According to that theory a person is more likely to become criminal, if he or she has low self control (a simple example: someone wants to have a big yacht, but does not have the means to buy one—if the person cannot control herself—he or she might try to get the yacht (or the means for it) in an illegal way; whereas someone with high self-control will (more likely) either wait or deny himself that need).

BRITISH AND AMERICAN SUBCULTURAL THEORY

Following on from the Chicago School and Strain Theory, and also drawing on Edwin H. Sutherland's idea of differential association, subcultural theorists focused on small cultural groups fragmenting away from the mainstream to form their own values and meanings about life. Some of these groups, especially from poorer areas where opportunities were scarce, might adopt criminal values and meanings. British subcultural theorists focused more heavily on the issue of class, where some criminal activities were seen as 'imaginary solutions' to the problem of belonging to a subordinate class.

A further study by the Chicago school looked at gangs and the influence of the inter action of gang leaders under the observation of adults. The findings were described as being unreliable due to the observation techniques.

TYPES AND DEFINITIONS OF CRIME

Both the Positivist and Classical Schools take a consensus view of crime – that a crime is an act that violates the basic values and beliefs of society. Those values and beliefs are manifested as laws that society agrees upon. However, there are two types of laws:

Natural laws are rooted in core values shared by many cultures. Natural laws protect against harm to persons (e.g. murder, rape, assault) or property (theft, larceny, robbery), and form the basis of common law systems.

Statutes are enacted by legislatures and reflect current cultural mores, albeit that some laws may be controversial, e.g. laws that prohibit marijuana use and gambling. Marxist Criminology, Conflict Criminology and Critical Criminology claim that most relationships between State and citizen are non-consensual and, as such, criminal law is not necessarily representative of public beliefs and wishes: it is exercised in the interests of the ruling or dominant class. The more right wing criminologies tend to posit that there is a consensual social contract between State and citizen.

Therefore, definitions of crimes will vary from place to place, in accordance to the cultural norms and mores, but may be broadly classified as:

blue-collar crime;

corporate crime;

organised crime;

political crime;

public order crime;

state crime;

state-corporate crime;

white-collar crime.

Educational Programs

There is now a huge number of undergraduate and postgraduate criminology degrees available around the world. The present popularity of such degrees may in part be due to criminal and police television dramas that capture people's imaginations, but could also be because of growing awareness as to the continuing importance of issues relating to law, rules, compliance, politics, terrorism, security, forensic science, the media, deviance, and punishment.

3

SOCIOLOGY OF CULTURE AND THEORETICAL PERSPECTIVES

INTRODUCTION

Sociology of culture," or "cultural sociology," is one of the most popular fields of sociology, particularly in the United States and Europe. Cultural sociology is a methodology that accounts for social life as an outcome of meaning or interpretation.

Cultural sociologists are primarily influenced by Max Weber. More than other fields of sociology, cultural sociologists are predisposed to humanistic investigation and postmodern analysis. Scientific investigation and the production of empirically verifiable analysis (especially in terms of testable theories) is considered taboo among many cultural sociologists.

While most fields of sociology are defined by their object of inquiry or dependent variable (for example, sociologists of law study of the variation in law), cultural sociology is a paradigm. The American Sociological Association section for the sociology of culture states that the sociology of culture is a "perspective" that "considers material products, ideas, and symbolic means and their relation to social behavior."

As a perspective on social life, those that do cultural sociology study all aspects of social life, including diverse topics such as racism, fascism, love, and trade associations.

Though sociologists of culture expend much energy refining and debating their conceptulizations of culture, modern sociologists of culture have generally adopted a traditionally anthropological conception of culture that takes culture as social structure and social practice.

Key figures in today's cultural sociology include Jeffrey Alexander, Mabel Berezin, Michele Lamont, Lynn Spielman, and Ann Swidler.

Demography

From Wikipedia, the free encyclopedia

Map of countries by population

Population growth showing projections for later this century

Demography is the scientific study of human population dynamics. It encompasses the study of the size, structure and distribution of populations, and how populations change over time due to births, deaths, migration and ageing. Demographic analysis can relate to whole societies or to groups defined by criteria such as education, nationality, religion and ethnicity.

Most countries' demography is regarded as a branch of either economics or sociology. **Formal demography** limits its object of study to the measurement of populations processes, while the more broad field of population studies also analyze the relationships between economic, social, cultural and biological processes influencing the population.

The term demographics is often used erroneously for demography, but refers rather to selected population characteristics as used in marketing or opinion research, or the demographic profiles used in such research.

Data and Methods

Demographers may rely on the use of large amounts of data, including census returns and vital statistics registers, or incorporate survey data using indirect estimation techniques.

The earliest modern census was carried out in the United States in 1790, although, the Scandinavian countries had earlier censuses.

In many countries, particularly in the developing countries, reliable demographic data is still difficult to obtain; census is often equated in the minds of the people with taxation, so the people scatter when a census taker comes around.

During the 1980s, for example, the population of Nigeria was widely estimated to be around 101 million people, before it was established to be as little as 89 million people (without adjustment for undercounting) in a census carried out in 1991.

Important Concepts

Important concepts in demography include:

- The **crude birth rate**, the annual number of live births per thousand people.
- The **general fertility rate**, the annual number of live births per 1000 women of childbearing age (often taken to be from 15 to 49 years old, but sometimes from 15 to 44).

- **Age-specific fertility** rates, the annual number of live births per 1000 women in particular age groups (usually age 15-19, 20-24 etc.)
- The **crude death rate**, the annual number of deaths per 1000 people.
- The **infant mortality rate**, the annual number of deaths of children less than 1 year old per thousand live births.
- The **expectation of life** (or life expectancy), the number of years which an individual at a given age can expect to live at present mortality levels.
- The **total fertility rate**, the number of live births per woman completing her reproductive life, if her childbearing at each age reflected current age-specific fertility rates.
- The **gross reproduction rate**, the number of daughters who would be born to a woman completing her reproductive life at current age-specific fertility rates.
- The **net reproduction ratio** is the expected number of daughters, per newborn prospective mother, who may or may not survive to and through the ages of childbearing.

Note that the crude death rate as defined above and applied to a whole population can give a misleading impression. For example, the number of deaths per 1000 people can be higher for developed nations than in less-developed countries, despite standards of health being better in developed countries. This is because developed countries have relatively more older people, who are more likely to die in a given year, so that the overall mortality rate can be higher even if the mortality rate at any given age is lower. A more complete picture of mortality is given by a life table which summarises mortality separately at each age. A life table is necessary to give a good estimate of life expectancy.

BASIC DEMOGRAPHIC EQUATION

Suppose that a country (or other entity) contains $Population_t$ persons at time t. What is the size of the population at time $t + 1$?

$Population_{t+1} = Population_t + Births_t - Deaths_t + Immigration_t - Emigration_t$

Net migration from time t to $t + 1$:

$Netmigration_{t+1} = Immigration_t - Emigration_t$

Natural increase from time t to $t + 1$

$Naturalincrease_{t+1} = Births_t - Deaths_t$

History

The *Natural and Political Observations ... upon the Bills of Mortality* (1662) of John Graunt contains a primitive form of life table. Mathematicians, such as Edmond Halley, developed the life table as the basis for life insurance mathematics. Richard Price was credited with the first textbook on life contingencies published in 1771. (ref: "Our Yesterdays: the History of the Actuarial Profession in North America, 1809-1979," by E.J. (Jack) Moorhead, FSA, (1/23/10 – 2/21/04), published by the Society of Actuaries as part of the profession's centennial celebration in 1989; followed later by Augustus de Morgan, 'On the Application of Probabilities to Life Contingencies', (1838). (ref: The History of Insurance, Vol 3, Edited by David Jenkins and Takau Yoneyama (1 85196 527 0): 8 Volume Set: (2000) Availability: Japan: Kinokuniya)

At the end of the 18th century, Thomas Malthus concluded that, if unchecked, populations would be subject to exponential growth. He feared that population growth would tend to outstrip growth in food production, leading to ever increasing famine and poverty (see Malthusian catastrophe); he is seen as the intellectual father of ideas of overpopulation and the limits to growth. Later more sophisticated and realistic models were presented by e.g. Benjamin Gompertz and Verhulst.

The Demographic Transition

Contrary to Malthus' predictions (though in line with his thoughts on moral restraint), natural population growth in most developed countries has diminished to close to zero, without being held in check by famine or lack of resources, as people in developed nations have shown a tendency to have fewer children. The fall in population growth has occurred despite large rises in life expectancy in these countries. This pattern of population growth, with slow (or no) growth in preindustrial societies, followed by fast growth as the society develops and industrialises, followed by slow growth again as it becomes more affluent, is known as the demographic transition.

Similar trends are now becoming visible in ever more developing countries, so that far from spiralling out of control, world population growth is expected to slow markedly in the next century, coming to an eventual standstill. The change is likely to be accompanied by major shifts in the proportion of world population in particular regions. The United Nations Population Division expects the absolute number of infants and toddlers in the world to begin to fall by 2015, and the number of children under 15 by 2025. Demographers at the International Institute for Applied Systems Analysis in Austria expect world population to peak at 9000 million by 2070. Throughout the 21st century, the average age of the population is likely to continue to rise.

SOCIOLOGY OF DEVIANCE

From Wikipedia, the free encyclopedia

Jump to: navigation, search

The *sociology of deviance* is the sociological study of deviant behavior, the recognized violation of cultural norms, and the creation and enforcement of those norms. The sociology of deviance is related to, but also distinct from the field of criminology.

CONTENTS

THEORIES

The field of deviance is primarily defined by the theories used to explain deviance.

Labeling Theory

Howard S. Becker, a leading sociologist in this field, theorized in 1963 that "social groups create deviance by making the rules whose infraction constitutes deviance." Labeling theory suggests that deviance is caused by the deviant person being negatively labeled, internalizing the label, and acting according to the label. For example, if a teacher labels a student as unruly, the student may internalize that label from the authority figure and behave unruly as if the labeling was a self-fulfilling prophecy. This theory, while very much a symbolic-interactionist theory, also has elements of conflict theory as the dominate group has the power to decide what is deviant and acceptable, and enjoys the power behind the labeling process. An example of this theory is a prison system that labels people convicted of theft, and because of this they start to view themselves as thieves.

Strain Theory (Sociology)

Strain Theory Table

Accepts Goals

Rejects Goals Accepts Means

Conformist

Ritualist *Rejects Means*

Innovator

RetreatistRobert K. Merton discussed deviance in terms of goals and means as part of his strain/anomie theory. He postulated that an individual's response to societal expectations and the means by which the individual pursued those goals were useful in understanding deviance. Acceptance of both goals and means is defined as **conformity** (e.g. founding a business to achieve the American goal of wealth and materialism). Acceptance of the goals and rejection of the means is described as **innovation**, which can be positive or negative (e.g. acquiring wealth by robbery would be negative, while inventing a new business method would be positive). Rejection of the goal and acceptance of the means is **ritualism**—going through the motions, such as the disillusioned Milton in the movie Office Space (although his ritualism later changed to a mix of innovation and rebellion).

Rejection of both the goal and means is **retreatism**—a homeless person is often cited as an example. **Rebellion** is a special case, where the individual rejects both the goal and means and actively attempts to replace them with other systems which are more acceptable. Anything other than conformity is a form of deviance from the accepted societal norms of behavior.

Differential Association

Also known as Social Learning Theory, it explains deviance as a learned behavior. The most important variables in this theory are the age of the learner of deviance, the quality of contact between the learner and the deviant role model, and the relationship between the learner and the deviant model. It does a great job of explaining how children grow up to become law-breakers or juvenile offenders, but it suffers from a paradox. If all deviance is learned from a teacher, and the teacher learned from their teacher, how did the first teachers learn to be deviant?

Functionalism

Functionalism views deviance as something needed by society. For one, deviance tests boundaries and also reaffirms social norms. Deviance also provides jobs for medicine, law enforcement, social workers, politicians, religious leaders, etc. The persistence of deviance is explained by the fact that deviance is important in adaptation, and because people who work with social control do not want to completely end deviance because it provides them jobs. According to Durkheim, society is based on people sharing common values (collective conscience) which form the basis for actions. However, in periods of change or social stress, the collective conscience may be weakened.

In this situation people may start to look after their own selfish interests rather than adhering to social values. Durkheim called this situation anomie. Hirschi was heavily influenced by Durkheim's concept of anomie suggests that if people are not 'controlled' by shared social values, then they look after their own short-term interests without concern for others. Hirschi turned around the question of 'why people commit crime?' to another, equally intriguing one: 'Why don't people commit crime?' Hirschi argued that criminal activity occurs when people's attachment to society is weakened in the some way.

Conflict Theory

Conflict theorists generally see deviance as a result of conflict between individuals and groups. The theoretical orientation contributes to labeling theory in that it explains that those with power create norms and label deviants. Deviant behavior is actions that do not go along with the socially prescribed worldview of the powerful, and is often a result of the present social structure preventing the minority group access to scarse resources.

Since it explains deviance as a reaction due to conflict between groups and individuals due to scarse resources, it does a great job of explaining deviance by poor citizens, etc. However, it does not do such an excellent job in explaining white-collar crime.

Subculture

Subcultures can use deviance as a way from differentiating themselves from main stream society. This can be through clothing, tattoos, hair styles ect (for example punks) through to violent criminal behaviour (criminal gangs). Deviance therefore provides members of the subculture with a sense of common identity. It is interesting to note that members of a subculture are still following norms, just different norms from the rest of society. Norms are learned from other members of a subculture, a new member learns ways to act, dress, music to listen to ect. Deviance within a subculture will still be subjected to sanctions and possible expulsion from the subculture.

Medicalization of Deviance

Sociologists have also studied what is called the "medicalization" of deviance. Power of the ability to label deviants has greatly shifted from religious insititutions to healthcare institutions. This is evident by the increase of scientific and medical explanations for deviant behavior. For example, a person with a mental disorder under a religious explanation may would be considered to be possessed or blessed with supernatural powers, depending on the religious tradition.

However, the medicalization of deviance has caused mental problems and other health problems to be given medical explanations, and have impacted the roles in which a person plays. A person labeled as sick or mentally ill must then play the "sick role" where they are forgiven reasonable violations of norms so long as they are trying to receive medical attention from the healthcare professionals. Many sociologists have questioned the power in which mental health and other healthcare professionals have been able to maintain, and have even questioned the objectivity of the medical labels. Sociologists have also commented on the role medicine plays as an institution of social control much like the government.

Prosecution of Deviance

Sociologists have also observed that deviance is by law enforcement, but not prosecuted. Many incidents have been recorded as deviant acts but ignored by police so long as they do not harm unsuspecting citizens or do not call attention to themselves.

Media and Deviance

In Joel Best's book, *Random Violence: How We Talk about New Crimes and New Victims*, the author explains how society has evolved a "victim industry." Best compares our labeling and creation of victims to a witch-hunt. But instead of going around labeling and burning people as witches, we have started to frantically look for victims. Best also explains how the media distorts facts about violence and over-emphasizes its randomness and frequency.

Sociology of Disaster

From Wikipedia, the free encyclopedia

Jump to: navigation, search

Sociology of disaster is a special branch of sociology. The research is predominantly done in the United States, but also in Germany and Italy as well. Theoretically it includes not only local disasters, but catastrophies on a grand scale. One of the prominent researchers in this area is Robert A. Stallings.

Dramaturgy (Sociology)

From Wikipedia, the free encyclopedia

(Redirected from Dramaturgical sociology)

Jump to: navigation, search

For the theatre-related meaning of this word, see dramaturgy.

Dramaturgy is a sociological perspective stemming from the work of Erving Goffman. In dramaturgical sociology it is argued that human actions are dependent upon time, place, and audience.

Goffman suggested that our lives are dictated and set in society. He describes life as a "stage", and that individual humans are the actors that are upon it. Individuals play a "role" that is assigned to them through socialisation of norms and values. The norms, values and cultural information gives them a role such as a teenager, police officer or wife. This is done through the use of "scripts" that the actor performs to fulfill a role.

A useful way of understanding dramaturgy is to think of a waiter or waitress at a restaurant. Their main avenue of concern for him or her is "customer service". Even if a customer is rude, waiters and/or waitresses are expected to be polite—"the customer is always right"—as part of their job responsibilties. That same waiter or waitress speaks differently when going out to their break room. They may complain, mimic and discuss with their fellow peers how irritating and rude the customer is. In this example, the waiter/waitress acts a certain way when dealing with customers and acts a completely different way when with their fellow employees. Goffman referred to this as front stage/ back stage personalities.

Another example of dramaturgy is the case of Dennis Rader, the BTK Strangler. Rader appeared to be a religious family man, a "front stage" performance perhaps. But when not operating under that cover, he was a sadistic sexual killer who horrifically murdered 10 victims—i.e. his "back stage" persona.

Central concepts include stigma, stigmatized signs, "identity work", deviance disavowed, symptomatic actions, total institution, moral career.

Economic Sociology

From Wikipedia, the free encyclopedia

Jump to: navigation, search

Economic sociology is the sociological analysis of economic phenomena. As the earliest economists recognised, economic institutions are of profound importance to society as a whole and the social context affects the nature of local economic institutions. Karl Marx argued that economic forces were absolutely central to society and deeply influenced its social structures. The founding figures of sociology, such as Max Weber, similarly regarded economic processes as fundamental to the structure of society. Georg Simmel, particularly in his book "Philosophy of Money", was important in the early development of economic sociology, as was Emile Durkheim through "Division of Labor". Other important early contributions to economic sociology were made by people who are more usually thought of as economists, e.g. Thorstein Veblen and Joseph Schumpeter.

Later Marxist and other left-wing economic thought has focused on the social implications of consumerism and economic development within the system of economic relations that produce them.

Current economic sociology focuses particularly on the social consequences of economic exchanges, the social meanings they involve and the social interactions they facilitate or obstruct. Influential figures in modern economic sociology include Mark Granovetter, Harrison White, Paul DiMaggio, Richard Swedberg and Viviana Zelizer. To this may be added Amitai Etzioni, who has popularised the idea of socioeconomics, and Chuck Sabel and Wolfgang Streeck, who work in the tradition of political economy/sociology.

The focus on mathematical analysis and utility maximisation during the 20th century has led some to see economics as a discipline moving away from its roots in the social sciences. Many critiques of economics or economic policy begin from the accusation that abstract modelling is missing some key social phenomenon that needs to be addressed. In reply, many mainstream economists point out that such cultural and social arguments often seem to favour the interests of local monopolists and the already powerful.

Economists (Becker, 1976)have also attempted to bring economic approaches—in particular utility maximisation and game theory—to the analysis of social situations that are not obviously related to production or trade. This remains an active area of research, controversial both amongst economists and other social sciences.

Sociology of Education

From Wikipedia, the free encyclopedia

Jump to: navigation, search

The *sociology of education* is the study of how social institutions and individual experiences affect educational processes and outcomes. Education has always been seen as a fundamentally optimistic human endeavour [Schofield, 1999] characterised by aspirations for progress and betterment. By many in society, it is understood to be a means of overcoming handicaps, achieving greater equality and acquiring wealth and status for all [Sargent, 1994]. Education is perceived as a place where children can develop according to their unique needs and potentialities [Schofield, 1999]. It is also the best possible means of achieving greater equality in society [Sargent, 1994].

The purpose of education then, must be to develop every individual to their full potential and grant them a chance to achieve as much in life as their natural abilities allow. This promising vision, however, does not unfold into reality. The reality, according to many sociologists, is that education works towards a larger goal than that of the individual and its purpose is to maintain social stability, through the reproduction of inequality. What the goal of this stability is differs depending on which sociological perspective one uses to approach the issue.

CONTENTS

Educational Sociologists in Asia

Educational Sociologists in America

Educational Sociologists in Europe.

THEORETICAL PERSPECTIVES

Structural Functionalism

Structural functionalists believe that society tends towards equilibrium and social order. They see society like a human body, where key institutions work like the body's organs to keep the society/body healthy and well [Bessant & Watts, 2002]. Social health means the same as social order, and is guaranteed when everyone accepts the moral values of their society.

Hence, structural functionalists believe the purpose of key institutions, such as education, is to socialise young members of society. Socialisation is the process by which the new generation learns the knowledge, attitudes and values that they will need as citizens.

Although, this purpose is stated in the formal curriculum [NSW Board of Studies], it is mainly achieved through the hidden curriculum [Harper, 1997]. The hidden curriculum consists of a subtler, but nonetheless powerful, indoctrination of the norms and values of wider society.

Students learns these values because their behaviour at school is regulated [Durkheim in Sargent 1994] until they gradually internalise them and so accept them. Education must, however perform another function to keep society running smoothly.

As various jobs in society become vacant, they must be filled with the appropriate people. Therefore the other purpose of education is to sort and rank individuals for placement in the labour market [Munro, 1997]. Those with the greatest achievement will be trained for the most important jobs in society and in reward, be given the highest incomes. Those who achieve the least, will be given the least demanding jobs, and hence the least income.

According to Sennet and Cobb [in Sargent, 1994:238] however, "to believe that ability alone decides who is rewarded is to be deceived". Meighan [1997] agrees stating that large numbers of capable students from working class backgrounds fail to achieve satisfactory standards in school and therefore fail to obtain the status they deserve.

Jacob [2001] believes this is because the middle class cultural experiences that are provided at school may be contrary to the experiences they've had at home.

In other words working class children are not adequately prepared to cope at school. They are therefore "cooled out" [Foster, 1987:169] from school with the least qualifications, hence they get the least desirable jobs, and so remain working class. Sargent [1994] agrees with this cycle, stating that schooling supports continuity, which in turn support social order. Talcott Parsons [in Meighan, 1997:250] believed that this process, whereby some students were identified and labelled educational failures, "was a necessary activity which one part of the social system, education, performed for the whole".

Yet the structural functionalist perspective maintains that this social order, this continuity, is what most people desire [Bessant & Watts, 2002]. The weakness of this perspective here becomes evident. Why would the working class wish to stay the working class? Such an inconsistency demonstrates that another perspective may be more useful in examining the issue further.

CONFLICT THEORY

Education and Social Reproduction

The perspective of conflict theory, contrary to structural functionalist perspective, believes that society is full of vying social groups who have different access to life chances and gain different social rewards [Furze & Healy, 1997]. In other words power is in the hands of a few who use it to maintain their position by arranging society to their advantage. Relations in society are based on exploitation, oppression, domination and subordination [Sargent, 1994].

Although, this is a considerably more cynical picture of society, it is also more realistic than the previous idea that most people accept continuing inequality. Conflict theorists believe education is controlled by the state which is controlled by those with the power, and its purpose is to reproduce the inequalities already existing in society as well as legitimise 'acceptable' ideas which actually work to reinforce the privileged positions of the dominant group [Furze & Healy, 1997].

Connell and White [1989] state that the education system is as much an arbiter of social privilege as a transmitter of knowledge. Education achieves its purpose by maintaining the status quo, where working class children become working class adults, and middle class children become middle class adults.

This cycle occurs because the dominant group has, over time, closely aligned education with middle class values and aspirations, thus alienating people of other classes [Connell & White, 1997]. Indeed many teachers assume that students will have particular middle class experiences at home, and for many children this assumption isn't true [Jacob, 2001]. Many working class children are expected to help their parents after school and carry considerable domestic responsibilities in the home [Wilson & Wyn, 1987]. The demands of this domestic labour often make it difficult for them to find time to do all their homework and thus affects their performance at school. Where teachers have reduced the formality of regular study and integrated student's preferred way of working into the curriculum, they noted that particular students displayed strengths they had not been aware of before [Wilson & Wyn, 1987].

However, few teacher deviate from the traditional curriculum, and the curriculum conveys what constitutes knowledge as determined by the state–and those in power [Young in Sargent, 1994]. This knowledge isn't very meaningful to many of the working class, they do not see it serving any purpose [Jacob, 2002]. Wilson & Wyn [1987] state that the students realise there is no direct link between the subjects they are doing and their future in the labour market.

Anti-school values displayed by these children, are actually derived from their consciousness of their real interests. Sargent believes that for working class students, striving to succeed and absorbing the middle class values of school, is accepting their inferior social position in society [Sargent, 1994] as much as if they determined to fail. Fitzgerald [in Henry et al, 1988:143] states that "irrespective of their academic ability or desire to learn, students from poor families have relatively little chance of securing success".

On the other hand, for middle and especially upper class children, maintaining their superior position in society requires little effort. The federal government subsidises 'independent' private schools enabling the rich to obtain 'good education' by paying for it [Sargent, 1994]. With this 'good education', rich children perform better, achieve higher and obtain greater rewards. In this way, the continuation of privilege and wealth for the elite is made possible.

Once again the question is raised, why would working class people allow this to happen? Conflict theorists believe this social reproduction continues to occur because the whole education system is overlain with ideology provided by the dominant group. In effect, they perpetuate the myth that education is available to all to provide a means of achieving wealth and status. Anyone who fails, continues the myth, to achieve this goal has therefore only themself to blame [Sargent, 1994:234]. Wright [in Sargent, 1994:234] agrees, stating that "the effect of the myth is to stop them from seeing that their personal troubles are part of major social issues".

The duplicity is so successful that many parents endure appalling jobs for many years, believing that this sacrifice will enable their children to have opportunities in life that they did not have themselves [Wilson & Wyn, 1987]. These people who are poor and disadvantaged are victims of a societal confidence trick. They have been encouraged to believe that a major goal of schooling in to increase equality while, in reality, schools reflect society's intention to maintain the previous unequal distribution of status and power. [Fitzgerald, in Sargent, 1994] This perspective has been criticised for being deterministic and allowing no room for the agency of individuals.

STRUCTURE AND AGENCY

Bourdieu and Cultural Capital

This theory of social reproduction has been significantly theorised by Pierre Bourdieu. However Bourdieu as a social theorist has always been concerned with the dichotomy between the objective and subjective, or to put it another way, between structure and agency. Bourdieu has therefore built his theoretical framework around the important concepts of habitus, field and cultural capital.

These concepts are based on the idea that objective structures determine the probability of individuals' life chances, through the mechanism of the habitus where individuals internalise these structures. However, the habitus is also formed by, for example, an individual's position in various fields, their family and their everyday experiences. Therefore one's class position does not determine one's life chances but it does play an important part alongside other factors.

Bourdieu employed the concept of cultural capital to explore the differences in outcomes for students from different classes in the French education system. He explored the tension between the conservative reproduction and the innovative production of knowledge and experience [Harker, 1990:87]. He found that this tension is intensified by considerations of which particular cultural past and present is to be conserved and reproduced in schools. Bourdieu argues that it is the culture of the dominant groups, and therefore their cultural capital, which is embodied in schools, and that this leads to social reproduction [Harker, 1990:87].

The cultural capital of the dominant group, in the form of practices and relation to culture, is assumed by the school to be the natural and only proper type of cultural capital and is therefore legitimated. It thus demands "uniformly of all its students that they should have what it does not give" [Bourdieu in Swartz, 2000:209].

This legitimate cultural capital allows students who possess it to gain educational capital in the form of qualifications. Those students of less privileged classes are therefore disadvantaged. To gain qualifications they must acquire legitimate cultural capital, by exchanging their own (usually working-class) cultural capital [Harker, 1984:172]. This process of exchange is not a straight forward one, due to the class ethos of the less privileged students. Class ethos is described as the particular dispositions towards, and subjective expectations of, school and culture. It is in part determined by the objective chances of that class [Gorder, 1980:226].

This means, that not only is it harder for children to succeed in school due to the fact that they must learn a new way of 'being', or relating to the world, and especially, a new way of relating to and using language, but they must also act against their instincts and expectations.

The subjective expectations influenced by the objective structures located in the school, perpetuate social reproduction by encouraging less-privileged students to eliminate themselves from the system, so that fewer and fewer are to be found as one progresses through the levels of the system [Bourdieu, 1990:155]. The process of social reproduction is neither perfect nor complete [Harker, 1990:87], but still, only a small number of less-privileged students make it all the way to the top.

For the majority of these students who do succeed at school, they have had to internalise the values of the dominant classes and take them as their own, to the detriment of their original habitus and cultural values.

Therefore Bourdieu's perspective reveals how objective structures play a large role in determining the achievement of individuals at school, but allows for the exercise of an individual's agency to overcome these obstacles, although this choice is not without its penalties.

Environmental Sociology

From Wikipedia, the free encyclopedia

Jump to: navigation, search

Environmental sociology is typically defined as the study of societal-environmental interactions, or the relationships between modern societies and their biophysical environments.

Environmental sociologists study the factors that cause environmental problems, the societal impacts of those problems, as well as efforts to solve the problems. In addition, considerable attention is paid to the social processes by which certain environmental conditions become socially defined as problems.

Although, there was sometimes acrimonious debate between the constructivist and realist "camps" within environmental sociology in the 1990s, the two sides have found considerable common ground as both increasingly accept that while most environmental problems have a material "reality" they nonetheless become known only via human processes such as scientific knowledge, activists' efforts, and media attention.

In other words, most environmental problems have a "real" ontological status despite our knowledge/awareness of them stemming from social processes, processes by which various conditions are "constructed" as problems by scientists, activists, media and other social actors.

Correspondingly, environmental problems must all be understood via social processes, despite any material basis they may have external to the human. This interactiveness is now broadly accepted, but many aspects of the debate continue in contemporary research in the field.

SOCIOLOGY OF THE FAMILY

From Wikipedia, the free encyclopedia

Jump to: navigation, search

Sociology of the family is the study of the family unit from a sociological viewpoint. The examination is dominated by class, gender and ethnicity analysis. Further sociology of the family views the effect of social change on the family.

Included in this type of study are the number of children in the family, their relative ages, their racial and/or ethnic backgrounds, the economic level and mobility of the unit, the education levels of the family members, what spheres of life are important in and to the family unit, and all of the intereractions of the family unit, society, culture and with each other.

Sociology of families is also concerned with the diversity of family forms in contemporary societies in relation to ideology, gender differences, and state policies such as those concerned with marriage.

Sociology studies families and their formation, Sociology studies social change and trends surrounding the family such as,

- Increase in sole occupancy dwellings and smaller family sizes
- Average age of marriage being older
- Average number of children decreasing and first birth at later age
- The historical pattern of fertility. From baby boom to baby bust (instability)
- The ageing population. The trend towards greater life expectancy.

- Rising divorce rates and people who will never marry.

Sociology of the family examines the changing roles of family members. Each member is restricted by the sex roles of the traditional family, these roles such as the father as the worker and the mother as the homemaker are declining, the mother is becoming the supplementary provider and she retains the responsibilities of child rearing. Therefore the females' role in the labour force is "compatible with the demands of the traditional family".[2] Sociology studies the adaptation of the males role to caregiver as well as provider. The gender roles are increasingly interwoven.

CONTENTS

Marxist View of the Family

Contemporary society is controlled by capitalism. Women are oppressed by capitalism, therefore capitalism and women and the family are an interconnected group. As capitalism extends its grip on the world, women, the family and family values are decreasing in relevance. Traditional Marxist theory states the oppression exists from women's domestic labour being exploited.

With many of the world women suffering economic oppression, the family must be revised. A new form of family must be established that is classless and does not restrict its members to social roles of inferiority. Marxists believes this is only possible with the establishment of "true socialism". Therefore the contemporary family must forget social institutions and capitalist family values as it overcomes economic oppression and ideological oppression.

Examples of the relationship between the family and capitalism :

- Children are socialised to be good workers, primed for exploitation
- The family undermines the class struggle; the family members fight and are divided
- Oppressed workers can release discontent and be the boss in the family, but not at work
- Capitalist support the existence of many smaller families to increase consumerism
- Women are the reserve army of labour that undercut males wages and keeps males in their low-paying jobs
- The families' unpaid labour in the home is in capitalisms' interest.

Contemporary society must disregard social institutions and current family values as they only symbolise oppression and exploitation.

FUNCTIONALISM (SOCIOLOGY)

From Wikipedia, the free encyclopedia

Jump to: navigation, search

The article is about functionalism in sociology; for other uses, see functionalism.

In the social sciences, specifically sociology and sociocultural anthropology, **functionalism**, also called **functional analysis**, is a sociological philosophy that originally attempted to explain social institutions as collective means to fill individual biological needs. Later, it came to focus on the ways in which social institutions fill social needs, especially social stability. Functionalism is based around a number of key concepts. Firstly, society is viewed as a system – a collection of interdependent parts, with a tendency to equilibrium. Secondly, there are functional requirements that must be met in a society for its survival (such as reproduction of the population). Thirdly, phenomena are seen to exist because they serve a function [Holmwood, 2005:87]. Along with conflict theory and interactionism, functionalism is one of the three major sociological traditions. The theory is associated with Émile Durkheim and more recently with Talcott Parsons.

CONTENTS

Early functionalism

Parsons and Functionalism

Merton & Functionalism

Criticisms

Other theories

Famous functionalists.

EARLY FUNCTIONALISM

Many functionalists argue that social institutions are functionally integrated to form a stable system and that a change in one institution will precipitate a change in other institutions; this is expressed by Durkheim and others as an "organic analogy." **Structural functionalism**, which was developed by Meyer Fortes and Edward Evan Evans-Pritchard, is the main theory of this concept. The whole of functionalism, originating as an alternative to historical explanations, was one of the first twentieth century anthropological theories, until it was superseded by structural functional analysis or **structural-functionalism**.(see Kingsley Davis and Wilbert moore). Prior to social movements in the 1960s, functionalism was the dominant view in sociological thinking; after that time conflict theory challenged the current society, which functionalist theory defended.

Parsons and Functionalism

Parsons was heavily influenced by Durkheim and Weber, synthesising much of their work into his theory. Parsons' wanted to develop a 'grand theory' of society, but he began by examining the individual and their actions. He stated that "the social system is made up of the actions of individuals" [Parsons & Shills, 1976:190]. His starting point was the interaction between two individuals [Parsons, 1961:41]. Those individual were faced with a variety of choices about how they might act. However, those choices are influenced and constrained by a number of physical and social factors [Craib, 1992:40].

Parsons determined that each individual has expectations of the other's action and reaction to their own behaviour, and that these expectations are derived from the accepted norms and values of the society which they inhabit [Parsons, 1961:41]. These social norms are generally accepted and agreed upon [Gingrich, 1999].

As the behaviours are repeated in more interactions and these expectations are entrenched or institutionalised a role is created. Parsons defines a role as the "normatively regulated, participating of a person in a concrete process of social interaction with specific, concrete role-partners" [1961;43-44]. Although, any individual (theoretically) can fulfill any role, they are expected to conform to the norms governing the nature of the role they fulfill [Cuff & Payne, 1984:44]. Furthermore, one person fulfills many different roles at the same time. In one sense an individual can be seen to be a "composition" [Parsons & Shills, 1976:190] of the roles in which they inhabit. Certainly today, when asked to describe themselves most people would answer with reference to their roles in society.

Parsons then developed the idea of roles into collectivities of roles that complemented each other in fulfilling functions for society [Parsons, 1961:41]. Some of the roles are bound up in institutions and social structures, such as economic, educational, legal, and even gender structures. These structures are functional in the sense they assist society to operate [Gingrich, 1999], and fulfill its functional needs so that the society runs smoothly.

A society where there is no conflict, where everyone knows what is expected of them, and where these expectations are constantly being met, is in a perfect state of equilibrium. The key processes for Parsons in attaining this equilibrium are socialisation and social control. Socialisation is important because it is the mechanism for transferring the accepted norms and values of a society to the individuals within the system. Perfect socialisation occurs when these norms and vales are completely internalised, that is they become part of the individual's personality [Ritzer, 1983:196].

Parsons states, "this point, it should be made clear, is independent of the sense in which individual are concretely autonomous or creative rather than 'passive' or 'conforming', for individuality and creativity, are to a considerable extent, phenomena of the institutionalisation of expectations" [1961:38], that is they are culturally constructed characteristics. Socialisation is supported by the positive and negative sanctioning of role behaviours which do or do not meet these expectations [Cuff & Payne, 1984:46]. A punishment could be informal, such as a snigger or gossip, or more formalised through institutions such as prisons and mental institutions. If these two processes were perfect then society would become static and unchanging, and in reality this is unlikely to occur for long.

Parsons recognises this, stating that he treats "the structure of the system as problematic and subject to change" [1961:37] and that his concept of the tendency towards equilibrium "does not imply the empirical dominance of stability over change" [1961:39]. He does however believe that these changes occur in a relatively smooth way. Individuals in interaction with changing situations adapt through a process of "role bargaining" [Gingrich, 1991].

Once the roles are established, they create norms that guide further action and are thus institutionalised, creating stability across social interactions. Where the adaptation process cannot adjust, due to sharp shocks or immediate radical change, structural dissolution occurs and either new structures (and therefore a new system) are formed, or the society dies. This model of social change has been described as a "moving equilibrium" [Gingrich, 1991], and does emphasise a desire for social order.

MERTON & FUNCTIONALISM

Merton was a functionalist and he fundamentally agreed with Parsons' theory, however he acknowledged that it was problematic, believing that it was too generalised [Holmwood, 2005:100]. Merton tended to emphasise middle-range theory rather than a grand theory, meaning that he was able to deal specifically with some of the limitations in Parsons' theory. He identified 3 main limitations: functional unity, universal functionalism and indispensability [Ritzer in Gingrich, 1999]. He also developed the concept of deviance and made the distinction between manifest and latent functions.

Merton criticised functional unity, saying that not all parts of a modern, complex society work for the functional unity of society. Some institutions and structures may have other functions, and some may even be generally dysfunctional, or be functional for some while being dysfunctional for others. This is because not all structures are functional for society as a whole. Some practices are only functional for a dominant individual or a group [Holmwood, 2005:91]. Here Merton introduces the concepts of power and coercion into functionalism and identifies the sites of tension which may lead to struggle or conflict. Merton states that by recognising and examining the dysfunctional aspects of society we can explain the development and persistence of alternatives. Thus, as Holmwood states, "Merton explicitly made power and conflict central issues for research within a functionalist paradigm" [2005:91].

Merton also noted that there may be functional alternatives to the institutions and structures currently fulfilling the functions of society. This means that the institutions that currently exist are not indispensable to society. Merton states that "just as the same item may have multiple functions, so may the same function be diversely fulfilled by alternative items" [cited in Holmwood, 2005:91]. This notion of functional alternatives is important because it reduces the tendency of functionalism to imply approval of the status quo.

Merton's theory of deviance is derived from Durkheim's idea of anomie. It is central in explaining how internal changes can occur in a system. For Merton, anomie means a discontinuity between cultural goals and the accepted methods available for reaching them.

Merton believes that there are 5 situations facing an actor. Conformity occurs when an individual has the means and desire to achieve the cultural goals socialised into him. Innovation occurs when an individual strives to attain the accepted cultural goals but chooses to do so in novel or unaccepted method.

Ritualism occurs when an individual continues to do things as proscribed by society but forfeits the achievement of the goals. Retreatism is the rejection of both the means and the goals of society and rebellion is a combination of the rejection of societal goals and means and a substitution of other goals and means. Thus it can be seen that change can occur internally in society through either innovation or rebellion. It is true that society will attempt to control these individuals and negate the changes, but as the innovation or rebellion builds momentum, society will eventually adapt or face dissolution.

The last of Merton's important contributions to functionalism was his distinction between manifest and latent functions. Manifest functions refer to the conscious intentions of actors; latent functions are the objective consequences of their actions, which are often unintended [Holmwood, 2005:90].

Merton used the example of the Hopi rain dance to show that sometimes an individual's understanding of their motive for an action may not fully explain why that action continues to be performed. Sometimes actions fulfill a function of which the actor is unaware, and this is the latent function of an action.

Criticisms

In the 1960s, functionalism was criticized for being unable to account for social change or structuralist contradictions and conflict and thus often called "consensus theory." The refutation of the second criticism of functionalism, that it is static and has no concept of change, has already been articulated above, concluding that while Parsons' theory allows for change, it is an orderly process of change [Parsons, 1961:38], a moving equilibrium. Therefore referring to Parsons' theory of society as static is inaccurate.

It is true that it does place emphasis on equilibrium and the maintenance or quick return to social order, but this is a product of the time in which Parsons' was writing. This was post-World War II, and the start of the cold war. Society was in upheaval and fear abounded. At the time social order was crucial, and this is reflected in Parsons' tendency to promote equilibrium and social order rather than social change.

Furthermore, Durkheim used a radical form of guild socialism along with functionalist explanations. Also, Marxism, while acknowledging social contradictions, still uses functionalist explanations.

Parsons' evolutionary theory describes the differentiation and reintegration systems and subsystems and thus at least temporary conflict before reintegration (ibid). "The fact that functional analysis can be seen by some as inherently conservative and by others as inherently radical suggests that it may be *inherently* neither one nor the other." (Merton 1957: 39)

Stronger criticisms include the epistemological argument that functionalism is teleological, that is it attempts to describe social institutions solely through their effects and thereby does not explain the cause of those effects. However, Parsons drew directly on many of Durkheim's concepts in creating his theory. Certainly Durkheim was one of the first theorists to explain a phenomena with reference to the function it served for society. He said, "the determination of function is necessary for the complete explanation of the phenomena" [cited in Coser, 1977:140].

However Durkheim made a clear distinction between historical and functional analysis, saying, "when the explanation of a social phenomenon is undertaken, we must seek separately the efficient cause which produces it and the function it fulfills" [cited in Coser, 1977:140]. If Durkheim made this distinction, then it is unlikely that Parsons did not. However Merton does explicitly state that functional analysis does not seek to explain why the action happened in the first instance, but why it continues or is reproduced. He says that "latent functions go far towards explaining the continuance of the pattern" [cited in Elster, 1990:130, emphasis added]. Therefore it can be argued that functionalism does not explain the original cause of a phenomena with reference to its effect, and is therefore, not teleological.

Another criticism describes the ontological argument that society can not have "needs" as a human being does, and even if society does have needs they need not be met. Anthony Giddens argues that functionalist explanations may all be rewritten as historical accounts of individual human actions and consequences.(see Structuration theory). (ibid)

A further criticism directed at functionalism is that it contains no sense of agency, that individuals are seen as puppets, acting as their role requires. Yet Holmwood states that the most sophisticated forms of functionalism are based on "a highly developed concept of action" [2005:107], and as was explained above, Parsons took as his starting point the individual and their actions. His theory did not however articulate how these actors exercise their agency in opposition to the socialisation and inculcation of accepted norms. As has been shown above, Merton addressed this limitation through his concept of deviance, and so it can be seen that functionalism allows for agency. It cannot, however, explain why individuals choose to accept or reject the accepted norms, why and in what circumstances they choose to exercise their agency, and this does remain a considerable limitation of the theory.

Further criticisms have been levelled at functionalism by proponents of other social theories, particularly conflict theorists, marxists, feminists and postmodernists. Conflict theorists criticised functionalism's concept of systems as giving far too much weight to integration and consensus, and neglecting independence and conflict [Holmwood, 2005:100]. Lockwood [in Holmwood, 2005:101], in line with conflict theory, suggested that Parsons' theory missed the concept of system contradiction. He did not account for those parts of the system that might have tendencies to mal-integration. According to Lockwood, it was these tendencies that come to the surface as opposition and conflict among actors. However Parsons' thought that the issues of conflict and cooperation were very much intertwined and sought to account for both in his model [Holmwood, 2005:103]. In this however he was limited by his analysis of an 'ideal type' of society which was characterised by consensus. Merton, through his critique of functional unity, introduced into functionalism an explicit analysis of tension and conflict.

Marxism which was revived soon after the emergence of conflict theory, criticised professional sociology (functionalism and conflict theory alike) for being partisan to advanced welfare capitalism [Holmwood, 2005:103]. Gouldner [in Holmwood, 2005:103] thought that Parsons' theory specifically was an expression of the dominant interests of welfare capitalism, that it justified institutions with reference to the function they fulfill for society.

It may be that Parsons' work implied or articulated that certain institutions were necessary to fulfill the functional prerequisites of society, but whether or not this is the case, Merton explicitly states that institutions are not indispensable and that there are functional alternatives. That he does not identify any alternatives to the current institutions does reflect a conservative bias, which as has been stated before is a product of the specific time that he was writing in.

As functionalism's prominence was ending, feminism was on the rise, and it attempted a radical criticism of functionalism. It believed that functionalism neglected the suppression of women within the family structure. Holmwood [2005:103] shows, however, that Parsons did in fact describe the situations where tensions and conflict existed or were about to take place, even if he didn't articulate those conflicts. Some feminists agree, suggesting that Parsons' provided accurate descriptions of these situations. [Johnson in Holmwood, 2005:103].

On the other hand, Parsons recognised that he had oversimplified his functional analysis of women in relation to work and the family, and focused on the positive functions of the family for society and not on its dysfunctions for women. Merton, too, although addressing situations where function and dysfunction occurred simultaneously, lacked a "feminist sensibility" [Holmwood, 2005:103], although I repeat this was likely a product of the desire for social order.

Postmodernism, as a theory, is critical of claims of truth. Therefore the idea of grand theory that can explain society in all its forms is treated with skepticism at the least. This critique is important because it exposes the danger that grand theory can pose, when not seen as a limited perspective, as one way of understanding society.

Jeffrey Alexander (1985) sees functionalism as a broad school rather than a specific method or system, such as Parson's, which is capable of taking equilibrium (stability) as a reference-point rather than assumption and treats structural differentiation as a major form of social change. "The name 'functionalism' implies a difference of method or interpretation that does not exist." (Davis 1967: 401) This removes the determinism criticized above. Cohen argues that rather than needs a society has dispositional facts: features of the social environment that support the existence of particular social institutions but do not cause them. (ibid)

OTHER THEORIES

Structural functionalism, a theoretical concept developed by other anthropologists like Claude Lévi-Strauss and Edmund Leach, takes the view that society consists of parts (e.g. police, hospitals, schools, and farms), each of which have their own functions and work together to promote social stability. Structural-functionalism was the dominant perspective of cultural anthropologists and rural sociologists between World War II and the Vietnam War.

A social function is "the contribution made by any phenomenon to a larger system of which the phenomenon is a part." (Hoult 1969: 139) This technical usage is not the same as the popular idea of a function as an "event/occasion" or a duty, responsibility, or occupation.

A distinction, first made by Robert K. Merton, is made between manifest and latent functions (Marshall 1994: 190-1) and also between functions with positive (functional or positively functional) and negative (dysfunctional) effects (Hoult 1969: 139).

"Any statement explaining an institution as being 'functional or 'dysfunctional' for men [sic] could readily be translated with no loss of meaning into one that said it was 'rewarding' or 'punishing.'" (Homans 1962:33-4).

Functional alternative (also functional equivalent or functional substitute) indicates that, "just as the same item may have multiple functions, so may the same function be diversely fulfilled by alternative items." (Merton 1957: 33-4) The concept may serve as an antidote to "the gratuitous assumption of the functional indispensability of particular social structures."

THEORIES AND SOCIOLOGY OF THE HISTORY OF SCIENCE

From Wikipedia, the free encyclopedia

(Redirected from Sociology of the history of science)

Jump to: navigation, search.

History of Science Background Theories/Sociology

HistoriographyPseudoscience By era. In early culturesin Classical AntiquityIn the Middle Ages. In the Renaissance Scientific Revolution By topic Natural sciences Astronomy BiologyChemistry Ecology Geography Physics Social sciences Economics Linguistics Political Science Psychology Sociology

Technology Agricultural science Computer science Materials science Medicine Navigational pages Time lines Portal Categories.

The sociology and philosophy of science, as well as the entire field of science studies, have in the 20th century been preoccupied with the question of large-scale patterns and trends in the development of science, and asking questions about how science "works" both in a philosophical and practical sense.

CONTENTS

SCIENCE AS A SOCIAL ENTERPRISE

Science as a social enterprise has been developing exponentially for the past few centuries. In antiquity, the few people who were able to engage in natural inquiry were either wealthy themselves, had rich benefactors, or had the support of a religious community. In contrast, today there are more scientists alive now than have lived in all previous times. Scientific research has tremendous government support and also ongoing support from the private sector. Available methods of communication have improved tremendously over time. Instead of waiting months or years for a hand-copied letter to arrive, today scientific communication can be practically instantaneous. Earlier, most natural philosophers worked in relative isolation, due to the difficulty and slowness of communication. Still, there was a considerable amount of cross-fertilization between distant groups and individuals.

Nowadays, almost all modern scientists participate in a scientific community, hypothetically global in nature (though often based around a relatively few number of nations and institutions of stature), but also strongly segregated into different fields of study. The scientific community is important because it represents a source of established knowledge which, if used properly, ought to be more reliable than personally acquired knowledge of any given individual.

The community also provides a feedback mechanism, often in the form of practices such as peer review and reproducibility. Most items of scientific content (experimental results, theoretical proposals, or literature reviews) are reported in scientific journals and are hypothetically subjected to the scrutiny of their peers, though a number of scholarly critics from both inside and outside the scientific community have, in recent decades, began to question the effect of commercial and government investment in science on the peer review and publishing process, as well as the internal disciplinary limitations to the scientific publication process.

A major development of the Scientific Revolution was the foundation of scientific societies: Academia Secretorum Naturae (Accademia dei Segreti, the Academy of the Mysteries of Nature) can be considered the first scientific community; founded in Naples 1560 by Giambattista della Porta. The Academy had an exclusive membership rule: discovery of a new law of nature was a prequisite for admission. It was soon shut down by Pope Paul V under suspicion of sorcery.

The Academia Secretorum Naturae was replaced by the Accademia dei Lincei, founded in Rome 1603, included Galileo as a member, but failed upon his condemnation in 1633. The Accademia del Cimento, Florence 1657, lasted 10 years. The Royal Society of London, 1660 to the present day, brought together a diverse collection of scientists to discuss theories, conduct experiments, and review each other's work. The Académie des Sciences was created as an institution of the government of France 1666, meeting in the King's library. The Akademie der Wissenschaften began in Berlin 1700.

Early scientific societies provided valuable functions, including a community open to and interested in empirical inquiry, and also more familiar with and more educated about the subject. In 1758, with the aid of his pupils, Lagrange established a society, which was subsequently incorporated as the Turin Academy.

Much of what is considered the modern institution of science was formed during its professionalization in the 19th century. During this time the location of scientific research shifted primarily to universities, though also to some extent it also became a standard component of industry as well. In the early years of the twentieth century, especially after the role of science in the first World War, governments of major industrial nations began to invest heavily in scientific research.

This effort was dwarfed by the funding of scientific research undertaken by all sides in World War II, which produced such "wonder weapons" as radar, rocketry, and the atomic bomb. During the Cold War, a large amount of government resources were poured into science by the USA, USSR, and many European powers. It was during this time that ARPA funded nationwide computer networks of networks, one of them eventually under the internet protocol. In the post-Cold War era, a decline in government funding from many countries has been met with an increase of industrial and private investment. The funding of science is a major factor in its historical and global development, as though science is hypothetically international in scope, in a practical sense it has usually centered around wherever it could find the most funding.

Early scientific societies provided valuable functions, including a community open to and interested in empirical inquiry, and also more familiar with and more educated about the subject.

Major Events in the History of Scientific Communication

Gutenberg-era printing presses allowed the rapid spread of new ideas across 15th and 16th century Europe.

- The cave paintings depicted events, with no commentary. From 40,000 BC to 15,000 BC.
- The Ishango Bone dated 25,000 years ago could only show tallies in mathematical notation.
- The clay tablets of Mesopotamia show the *scale* of the commentary or the information: the argument and logic of a discovery would be limited to what fit on the tablet. From late 4th millennium onwards.
- Poetry and rhyme allowed people to remember memorable events more easily. For example, the Chinese generation names are taken from a poem selected by each family.
- The parchment and paper scrolls which arose in Greek and in Chinese culture could start to contain

the history and development of ideas and discoveries. Parchment was invented in Pergamon in the 2nd century BC, while the maunfacture of paper was described for the first time in 105 AD in China. It was brought to Western world only in the 13th century.

- The codex or book of medieval times allowed *random access* to specific passages. The systematic printing and production of books could then allow the systematic production of new ideas. From late 1st century onwards.
- By the twentieth century, the scale and scope of scientific work allowed collaboration of researchers and the definition of consistent protocols for this collaboration in scientific work.

POLITICAL SUPPORT

One of the basic requirements for a scientific community is the existence and approval of a political sponsor; in England, the Royal Society operates under the aegis of the monarchy; in the US, the National Academy of Sciences was founded by Act of Congress; etc.

Otherwise, when the basic elements of knowledge were being formulated, the political rulers of the respective communities could choose to arbitrarily either support or disallow the nascent scientific communities.

For example, Alhazen had to feign madness to avoid execution. The polymath Shen Kuo lost political support, and could not continue his studies until he came up with discoveries that showed his worth to the political rulers. The admiral Zheng He could not continue his voyages of exploration after the emperors withdrew their support.

Another famous example was the suppression of the work of Galileo, and before him, Giordano Bruno, burned at the stake (though for his views on theology rather than cosmology); by the twentieth century, Galileo would be pardoned.

Patterns in the History of Science

One of the major preoccupations with those interested in the history of science is whether or not it displays certain patterns or trends, usually along the question of change between one or more scientific theories. Generally speaking, there have historically been three major models adopted in various forms within the philosophy of science.

Three models of change in scientific theories, depicted graphically to reflect roughly the different views associated with Karl Popper, Thomas Kuhn, and Paul Feyerabend.

The first major model, implicit in most early histories of science and generally a model put forward by practicing scientists themselves in their textbook literature, is associated with the criticisms of logical positivism by Karl Popper (1902-1994) from the 1930s. Popper's model of science is one in which scientific progress is achieved through a falsification of incorrect theories and the adoption instead of theories which are progressively closer to truth.

In this model, scientific progress is a linear accumulation of facts, each one adding to the last. In this model, the physics of Aristotle (384 BC - 322 BC) was simply subsumed by the work of Isaac Newton (1642-1727) (classical mechanics), which itself was eclipsed by the work of Albert Einstein (1879-1955) (Relativity), and later the theory of quantum mechanics (established in 1925), each one more accurate than the last.

A major challenge to this model came from the work of the historian and philosopher Thomas Kuhn (1922-1996) in his work *The Structure of Scientific Revolutions* published in 1962. Kuhn, a former physicist, argued against the view that scientific progress was linear, and that modern scientific theories were necessarily just more accurate versions of theories of the past. Rather, Kuhn's version of scientific development consisted of dominant structures of thought and practices, which he called "paradigms", in which research went through phases of "normal" science ("puzzle solving") and "revolutionary" science (testing out new theories based on new assumptions, brought on by uncertainty and crisis in existing theories).

In Kuhn's model, different paradigms represented entirely different and incommensurate assumptions about the universe, and was uncertain about whether paradigms shifted in a way which necessarily relied upon greater attainment of truth. In Kuhn's view, Aristotle's physics, Newton's classical mechanics, and Einstein's Relativity were entirely different ways to think about the world; each successive paradigm defined what questions could be asked about the world and (perhaps arbitrarily) discarded aspects of the previous paradigm which no longer seemed applicable or important.

Kuhn claimed that far from merely building on the previous theory's accomplishments, each one essentially throws out the old way of looking at the universe, and comes up with its own vocabulary to describe it and its own guidelines for expanding knowledge within the new paradigm.

Kuhn's model met with much suspicion from scientists, historians, and philosophers. Some scientists felt that Kuhn went too far in divorcing scientific progress from truth;

many historians felt that his argument was too codified for something as polyvariant and historically contingent as scientific change; and many philosophers felt that the argument did not go far enough. The furthest extreme of such reasoning was put forth by the philosopher Paul Feyerabend (1924-1994), who argued that there were no consistent methodologies used by all scientists at all times which allowed certain forms of inquiry to be labeled "scientific" in a way which made them different from any other form of inquiry, such as witchcraft.

Feyerabend argued harshly against the notion that falsification was ever truly followed in the history of science, and noted that scientists had long undertaken practices to arbitrarily consider theories to be accurate even if they failed many sets of tests. Feyerabend argued that a pluralistic methodology should be undertaken for the investigation of knowledge, and noted that many forms of knowledge which were previously thought to be "non-scientific" were later accepted as a valid part of scientific canon.

Many other theories of scientific change have been proposed over the years with various changes of emphasis and implications. In general, though, most float somewhere between these three models for change in scientific theory, the connection between theory and truth, and the nature of scientific progress.

The Nature of Scientific Discovery

Individual ideas and accomplishments are among the most famous aspects of science, both internally and in larger society. Prolific figures like Sir Isaac Newton, or "breakthrough" thinkers like Albert Einstein are often celebrated as geniuses and heroes of science. Popularizers of science, including the news media and scientific biographers, contribute to this phenomenon. But many scientific historians emphasize the collective aspects of scientific discovery, and de-emphasize the importance of the "Eureka!" moment.

A detailed look at the history of science often reveals that the minds of great thinkers were "primed" with the results of previous efforts, and often arrive on the scene to find a crisis of one kind or another. For example, Einstein did not consider the physics of motion and gravitation in isolation. His major accomplishments solved a problem which had come to a head in the field only in recent years—empirical data showing that the speed of light was inexplicably constant, no matter the apparent speed of the observer. (See Michelson-Morley experiment.) Without this information, it is very unlikely that Einstein would have conceived of anything like relativity.

The question of who should get credit for any given "discovery" is often a source of some controversy. There are many "priority" disputes, in which multiple individuals or teams have competing claims over who discovered something first. Multiple simultaneous discovery is actually a surprisingly common phenomenon, perhaps largely explained by the idea that previous contributions (including the emergence of contradictions between existing theories, or unexpected empirical results) make a certain concept "ready" for discovery. Simple priority disputes are often a matter of documenting when certain experiments were performed, or when certain ideas were first articulated to colleagues or recorded in a fixed medium.

Many times the question of exactly which event is should qualify as the moment of discovery is difficult to answer. One of the most famous examples of this is the question of the discovery of oxygen. While Carl Wilhelm Scheele and Joseph Priestley were able to concentrate oxygen, in the laboratory and characterize its properties, they did not recognize it as a component of air.

Priestly, actually thought it was *missing* a hypothetical component of air, known as phlogiston, which air was supposed to absorb from materials that are being burned. It was only several years later that Antoine Lavoisier first conceived of the modern notion of oxygen—as a substance that is consumed from the air in the processes of burning and respiration.

By the late 20th Century, scientific research has become a large-scale effort, largely accomplished in institutional teams. The amount and frequency of inter-team collaboration has continued to increase, especially after the rise of the Internet, which is a central tool for the modern scientific community. This further complicates the notion of individual accomplishment in science.

SOCIOLOGY OF KNOWLEDGE

From Wikipedia, the free encyclopedia

Jump to: navigation, search

The *sociology of knowledge* is the study of the social origins of ideas, and of the effects prevailing ideas have on societies. (Compare history of ideas.)

The term first came into widespread use in the 1920s, when a number of German-speaking sociologists wrote extensively on it, notably Max Scheler, and Karl Mannheim with *Ideology and Utopia*. With the dominance of functionalism through the middle years of the 20th century, the sociology of knowledge tended to remain on the periphery of mainstream sociological thought. It was largely reinvented and applied much more closely to everyday life in the 1960s, particularly by Peter L. Berger and Thomas Luckmann in *The Social Construction of Reality* (1966) and is still central for methods dealing with qualitative understanding of human society. Compare *socially constructed reality*.

Although, very influential within modern sociology, the sociology of knowledge can claim its most significant impact on science more generally through its contribution to debate and understanding of the nature of science itself, most notably through the work of Thomas Kuhn in *The Structure of Scientific Revolutions* (see also: paradigm).

CONTENTS

SCHOOLS

Karl Mannheim

The German political philosophers Karl Marx (1818–1883) and Friedrich Engels (1820–1895) argued in *Die Deutsche Ideologie* (1846, *German Ideology*) and elsewhere that people's ideologies, including their social and political beliefs and opinions, are rooted in their class interests, and more generally in the social and economic circumstances in which they live: "It is men, who in developing their material inter-course, change, along with this their real existence, their thinking and the products of their thinking. Life is not determined by consciousness, but consciousness by life" (*Marx-Engels Gesamtausgabe* 1/5).

Under the influence of this doctrine, and of Phenomenology, the Hungarian-born German sociologist Karl Mannheim (1893–1947) gave impetus to the growth of the sociology of knowledge with his *Ideologie und Utopie* (1929, translated and extended in 1936 as *Ideology and Utopia*), although the term had been introduced five years earlier by the co-founder of the movement, the German philosopher and social theorist

Max Scheler (1874–1928), in *Versuche zu einer Soziologie des Wissens* (1924, *Attempts at a Sociology of Knowledge*). Mannheim feared that this interpretation could be seen to claim that all knowledge and beliefs are the products of socio-political forces since this form of relativism is self-defeating (if it is true, then it too is merely a product of socio-political forces and has no claim to truth and no persuasive force).

Mannheim believed that relativism was a strange mixture of modern and ancient beliefs in that it contained within itself a belief in an absolute truth which was true for all times and places (the ancient view most often associated with Plato) and condemned other truth claims because they could not achieve this level of objectivity (an idea gleaned from Marx).

Mannheim sought to escape this problem with the idea of 'relationism'. This is the idea that certain things are true only in certain times and places (a view influenced by pragmatism) however, this does not make them less true. Mannheim felt that a stratum of free-floating intellectuals (whom he claimed were only loosely anchored to the class structure of society) could most perfectly realise this form of truth by creating a "dynamic synthesis" of the ideologies of other groups.

PHENOMENOLOGICAL SOCIOLOGY

Based on the work of Edmund Husserl's philosophical phenomenology, Alfred Schutz proposed a micro-sociological approach also known as phenomenology. Schutz looked at the way in which ordinary members of society constitute and reconstitute the world in which they live; *life world.*

For Schutz, it was important to bracket one's taken-for-granted assumptions about the life in order to properly understand the life world of those being researched.

See: Holstein, J. A., & Gubrium, J. F. (1994). Phenomenology, ethnomethodology, and interpretive practice. In N.K. Denzin & Y. S. Lincoln (Eds.), *The handbook of qualitative research* (1st ed., pp. 262-272). Thousand Oaks, CA: Sage Publications.

MICHEL FOUCAULT

A particularly important strain of the sociology of knowledge is the criticism by Michel Foucault. In *Madness and Civilization*, 1961, he argued that conceptions of madness and what was considered "reason" or "knowledge" was itself subject to major culture bias—in this respect mirroring similar criticisms by Thomas Szasz, at the time the foremost critic of psychiatry, and himself now an eminent psychiatrist. A point where Foucault and Szasz agreed was that sociological processes played the major role in defining "madness" as an "illness" and prescribing "cures".

In *The Birth of the Clinic: An Archaeology of Medical Perception*, 1963, Foucault extended his critique to all of modern scientific medicine, arguing for the central conceptual metaphor of "The Gaze", which had implications for medical education, prison design, and the carceral state as understood today. Concepts of criminal justice and its intersection with medicine were better developed in this work than in Szasz and others, who confined their critique to current psychiatric practice.

Finally, in *The Order of Things*, 1966, and *The Archaeology of Knowledge*, 1969, Foucault introduced the abstract notions of mathesis and taxonomia. These, he claimed, had transformed 17th and 18th century studies of "general grammar" into modern "linguistics", "natural history" into modern "biology", and "analysis of wealth" into modern "economics". Not, claimed Foucault, without loss of meaning. The 19th century had transformed what knowledge was.

Perhaps Foucault's best-known and most controversial claim was that before the 18th century, "Man did not exist". The notions of humanity and of humanism were inventions or creations of this 19th century transformation.

Accordingly, a cognitive bias had been introduced unwittingly into science, by over-trusting the individual doctor or scientist's ability to see and state things objectively. This study still guides the sociology of knowledge and has been claimed to have sparked single-handedly much of postmodernism.

BRUNO LATOUR

Bruno Latour is a French sociologist of science best known for his books *We Have Never Been Modern, Laboratory Life,* and *Science in Action,* describing the process of scientific research from the perspective of social construction based on field observations of working scientists.

The Sociology of Mathematical Knowledge

Studies of mathematical practice and quasi-empiricism in mathematics are also rightly part of the sociology of knowledge, since they focus on the community of those who practice mathematics and their common assumptions. Since Eugene Wigner raised the issue in 1960 and Hilary Putnam made it more rigorous in 1975, the question of why fields such as physics and mathematics should agree so well has been debated. Proposed solutions point out that the fundamental constituents of mathematical thought, space, form-structure, and number-proportion are also the fundamental constituents of physics.

It is also worthwhile to note that physics is nothing but a modeling of reality, and seeing causal relationships governing repeatable observed phenomena, and much of mathematics, especially in relation to the growth of the calculus, has been developed precisely for the goal of developing these models in a rigorous fashion. Another approach is to suggest that there is no deep problem, that the division of human scientific thinking through using words such as 'mathematics' and 'physics' is only useful in their practical everyday function to categorify and distinguish.

Fundamental contributions to the sociology of mathematical knowledge have been made by Sal Restivo and David Bloor. Restivo draws upon the work of scholars such as Oswald Spengler (The Decline of the West, 1926), Raymond L. Wilder and Lesley A. White, as well as contemporary sociologists of knowledge and science studies scholars. David Bloor draws upon Ludwig Wittgenstein and other contemporary thinkers. They both claim that mathematical knowledge is socially constructed and has irreducible contingent and historical factors woven into it.

More recently Paul Ernest has proposed a social constructivist account of mathematical knowledge, drawing on the works of both of these sociologists.

Program Evaluation

From Wikipedia, the free encyclopedia

Jump to: navigation, search

Program evaluation is essentially a set of philosophies and techniques to determine if a program 'works'. It is a practice field that has emerged, particularly in the USA, as a disciplined way of assessing the merit, value, and worth of projects and programs. Evaluation became particularly relevant in the 1960s during the period of the Great Society social programs associated with the Kennedy and Johnson administrations. Extraordinary sums were invested in social programs, but the means of knowing what happened, and why were not available.

Behind the seemingly simple question of whether the program **works** are a host of other more complex questions. For example, the first question is, what is a program supposed to do? It is often difficult to define what a program is supposed to do, so indirect indicators may be used instead. For example schools are supposed to 'educate' people. But what does 'educate' mean? Give knowledge? Teach how to think? Give specific skills? If the exact goal cannot be defined well, it is difficult to indicate whether the program 'works'.

Another question about programs is, what else do they do? There may be unintended or unforeseen consequences of a program. Some consequences may be positive and some may be negative. These *un*intended consequences may be as important as the intended consequences. So evaluations should measure not just whether the program does what it should be doing, but what else it may be doing.

Perhaps the most difficult part of evaluation is determining whether it is the program itself that is doing something. There may be other events or processes that are really causing the outcome, or preventing the hoped for outcome. However, due to the nature of the program, many evaluations cannot determine whether it is the program itself, or something else, is the 'cause'.

One main reason that evaluations cannot determine causation involves self selection. That is, people select themselves to participate in a program. For example, in a jobs training program, some people decide to participate, and others, for whatever reason, do not participate. It may be that those who do participate are those who are most determined to find a job, or who have the best support resources, thus allowing them to participate and allowing them to find a job. The people who participate are somehow different from those who don't participate, and it may be the difference, not the program, that leads to a successful outcome for the participants, that is, finding a job.

If programs could, somehow, use random assignment, then they could determine causation. That is, if a program could randomly assign people to participate or to not participate in the program, then, theoretically, the group of people who participate would be the same as the group who did not participate, and an evaluation could 'rule out' other causes.

However, since most programs cannot use random assignment, causation cannot be determined. Evaluations can still provide useful information. For example, the outcomes of the program can be described. Thus the evaluation *can* say something like, "People who participate in program xyz were more likely to find a job, while people who did not participate were less likely to find a job."

If the program is fairly large, and there are many participants, and there is enough data, statistical analysis can be used sometimes to make a 'reasonable' case for the program by showing, for example, that other causes are unlikely.

Another approach is to use the evaluation to analyze the program process. So instead of focusing on the outcome (for example, did people in a jobs training program get jobs), the evaluation would focus on what the program was doing. For example, did people seem to learn the skills being taught? Did people stay in the program or did they drop out part way through? Were the teachers teaching appropriate skills? And so forth. This information could help how the program was operating.

People who do program evaluation can come from many different backgrounds, such as sociology, psychology, economics, social work or many other areas. Some graduate schools also have specific training programs for program evaluation.

TYPES OF EVALUATION

Program evaluation is often divided into types of evaluation.

Formative Evaluation occurs early in the program. The results are used to decide how the program is delivered, or what form the program will take. For example, an exercise program for elderly adults would seek to learn what activities are motivating and interesting to this group. These activities would then be included in the program.

Process Evaluation is concerned with how the program is delivered. It deals with things such as when the program activities occur, where they occur, and who delivers them.

In other words, it asks the question: Is the program being delivered as intended? An effective program may not yield desired results if it is not delivered properly.

Outcome Evaluation addresses the question of what are the results. It is common to speak of short-term outcomes and long-term outcomes. For example, in an exercise program, a short-term outcome could be a change knowledge about the health effects of exercise, or it could be a change in exercise behavior. A long-term outcome could be less likelihood of dying from heart disease.

PUBLIC SOCIOLOGY

From Wikipedia, the free encyclopedia

Jump to: navigation, search

Public sociology is an approach to the discipline which seeks to transcend the academy and engage wider audiences. Rather than being defined by a particular method, theory, or set of political values, public sociology may be understood as a *style* of sociology, a way of writing and a form of intellectual engagement. Michael Burawoy has contrasted it with *professional sociology*, a form of academic sociology that is concerned primarily with addressing other professional sociologists.

Burawoy and other promoters of public sociology seek to encourage the discipline to engage in explicitly public and political ways with issues stimulated by debates over public policy, political activism, the purposes of social movements, and the institutions of civil society. If there is a "movement" associated with public sociology, then, it is one that seeks to revitalize the discipline of sociology by leveraging its empirical methods and theoretical insights to engage in debates not just about what is or what has been in society, but about what society might yet be. Thus, many versions of public sociology have an undeniably normative and explicitly political character, typically leftist in nature.

CONTENTS

HISTORY

Debates over public sociology have rekindled questions concerning the extra-academic *purpose* of sociology. Public sociology raises questions about what sociology is and what its goals ought to (or even could) be. Such debates—over science and political advocacy, scholarship and public commitment—have a long history in American sociology and in American social science more generally. Historian Mark C. Smith, for instance, has investigated earlier debates over the purpose of social science in his book, *Social Science in the Crucible: The American Debate over Objectivity and Purpose,1918-1941* (Duke University Press, 1994). And Stephen Park Turner and Jonathan H. Turner showed how the discipline's search for a purpose, through dependence on external publics, has limited Sociology's potential in their book, *The Impossible Science: An Institutional Analysis of American Sociology* (Sage, 1990).

The term "public sociology" was first introduced by Herbert Gans, in a 1988 address entitled "Sociology in America: The Discipline and the Public." For Gans, primary examples of public sociologists included David Riesman, author of *The Lonely Crowd*, one of the best-selling books of sociology ever to be written, and Robert Bellah, the lead author of another best-selling work, *Habits of the Heart*. Some years later, sociologist Ben Agger wrote a book entitled *Public Sociology: From Social Facts to Literary Acts*. But it was Michael Burawoy's discussion of public sociology during his 2004 Presidency of the American Sociological Association that inspired a great deal of attention and debate.

Public Sociology Today

While there is no one definition of "public sociology" on which all sociologists agree, the term has come to be widely associated with Burawoy's promotion of it. Burawoy's personal statement for the ASA elections provides a succinct summary of his position:

"As mirror and conscience of society, sociology must define, promote and inform public debate about deepening class and racial inequalities, new gender regimes, environmental degradation, market fundamentalism, state and non-state violence. I believe that the world needs public sociology—a sociology that transcends the academy—more than ever. Our potential publics are multiple, ranging from media audiences to policy makers, from silenced minorities to social movements. They are local, global, and national. As public sociology stimulates debate in all these contexts, it inspires and revitalizes our discipline. In return, theory and research give legitimacy, direction, and substance to public sociology.

Teaching is equally central to public sociology: students are our first public for they carry sociology into all walks of life. Finally, the critical imagination, exposing the gap between what is and what could be, infuses values into public sociology to remind us that the world could be different." Wikipedia readers are encouraged to consult some of Burawoy's many papers on public sociology in order to learn more about his views.

Elsewhere, Burawoy has articulated a vision of public sociology that is consonant with the pursuit of democratic socialism. In *Critical Sociology*, Burawoy writes: "We might say that critical engagement with real utopias is today an integral part of the project of sociological socialism. It is a vision of socialism that places human society, or social humanity at its organizing center, a vision that was central to Marx but that was too often lost before it was again picked up by Gramsci and Polanyi (Burawoy, 2003b). If public sociology is to have a progressive impact it will have to hold itself continuously accountable to some such vision of democratic socialism."

In a slightly different vein, Burawoy and Jonathan VanAntwerpen of the University of California, Berkeley write that their departmental focus on public sociology aims to "turn, as C. Wright Mills would say, private concerns into public issues". The public sociology produced at Berkeley is an attempt to intervene in ongoing public debates over issues such as class and gender disparities and global inequality. Some of this work consists of attempts to refute high profile public scholarship in other fields (such as Herrnstein and Murray's *The Bell Curve*) and reclaim from non-sociologists the debate and explanation of sociological problems.

Likewise, the sociology department at the University of Minnesota also advocates claiming a larger role in public life: "Although good sociological research is often difficult to reduce to a sound-bite, sociologists have an important part to play in providing useful, accurate, and scientifically rigorous information to policy makers and community leaders".

Indeed, sociologists have not been alone in debating the "public role" of social science. Similar debates have occurred recently in the disciplines of economics, political science, anthropology, and history. In an effort to move these various disciplines "toward a more public social science," Craig Calhoun, the President of the Social Science Research Council, has encouraged sociologists and other social scientists to "ask better social science questions about what encourages scientific innovation, what makes knowledge useful, and how to pursue both these agendas, with attention to both immediate needs and longterm capacities. Calhoun has also entered the debate about public sociology, critically evaluating the project of public sociology while acknowledging its specific "promise," and arguing that "how sociology matters in the public sphere is vital to the future of the field".

Criticism

Of course, not all those who practice sociology either as public intellectuals or as academic professionals necessarily subscribe to the specific version of "public sociology" defended by Michael Burawoy (or even to any version of "public sociology" at all). And in the wake of Burawoy's 2004 Presidency of the American Sociological Association, which put the theme of public sociology in the limelight, the project of public sociology has been vigorously debated on the web, in conversations among sociologists, and in a variety of academic journals.

Specifically, Burawoy's vision of public sociology has been critiqued both by "critical" sociologists and by representatives of mainstream sociology. These various discussions of public sociology have been included in forums devoted to the subject in academic journals such as *Social Problems, Social Forces, Critical Sociology*, and the *British Journal of Sociology* [7]. These debates have produced both more interest in public sociology and more disagreement over what public sociology is and what its goals ought to be.

One of the most outspoken critics of public sociology is sociologist Mathieu Deflem of the University of South Carolina. Deflem argues that public sociology "is neither public nor sociology. Public sociology is not a plea to make sociology more relevant to the many publics in society nor to connect sociology democratically to political activity. Of course sociologists should be public intellectuals.

But they should be and can only be public intellectuals as practitioners of the science they practice, not as activists left or right. Yet public sociology instead is a quest to subsume sociology under politics, a politics of a specific kind, not in order to foster sociological activism but to narrow down the sociological discipline to activist sociology." (Deflem, Letter to the Editor, The Chronicle Review, 2004). Deflem also privately maintains SaveSociology.org in opposition to the advent of public sociology, and recently failed in his bid for election to an ASA Council position.

SOCIOLOGY OF RELIGION

From Wikipedia, the free encyclopedia

Jump to: navigation, search

The **sociology of religion** is primarily the study of the practices, social structures, historical backgrounds, development, universal themes, and roles of religion in society. There is particular emphasis on the recurring role of religion in nearly all societies on Earth today and throughout recorded history. Sociologists of religion attempt to explain the effects that society has on religion and the effects that religion has on society; in other words, their dialectical relationship.

CONTENTS

TYPOLOGY OF RELIGIOUS GROUPS

According to what is one common typology among sociologists, religious groups are classified as ecclesias, denominations, cults or sects. Note that sociologists give these words precise definitions which are different from how they are commonly used. Note especially that the words 'cult' and 'sect' as used by sociologists are free from prejudice, even though the popular use of these words is often pejorative.

History and Relevance Today

The classical, seminal sociological theorists of the late 19th and early 20th century were greatly interested in religion and its effects on society. These theorists include Émile Durkheim, Max Weber, and Karl Marx. Like Plato and Aristotle from Ancient Greece, and enlightenment philosophers from the 17th through 19th centuries, the ideas posited by these sociologists continue to be addressed today. More recent prominent sociologists of religion include Peter Berger, Michael Plekon, Rodney Stark, and Robert Wuthnow.

Despite the claims of many classical theorists and sociologists immediately after World War II, religion has continued to play a vital role in the lives of individuals worldwide. In America, for example, church attendance has remained relatively stable in the past 40 years. In Africa and South America, the emergence of Christianity has occurred at a startling rate. While Africa could claim roughly 10 million Christians in 1900, recent estimates put that number closer to 200 million. The rise of Islam as a major world religion, especially its new-found influence in the West, is another significant development. In short, presupposed secularization (the decline of religiosity) might seem to be a myth, depending on its definition and the definition of its scope—sociologists of religion still have much to study

Claims that the sociology of religion has no predictive ability (only descriptive) can be dismissed by the example above. Many sociologists predicted a rise in religiosity when cultural and philosophical figures were claiming "God is dead." Of course, many predicted the same thing as these figures. Nonetheless, the example stands. Other examples include:

–Peter Berger, noteworthy for predicting the "Culture Wars" of the late 20th century, especially its religious character.

–Sociologists who predicted the rise of fundamentalist Islam and its connection with terrorism.

Among many other predictive endeavors, sociologists of religion (notably Robert Wuthnow) are currently attempting to predict the success of U.S. federal funding of Faith-based charities.

THE VIEW OF RELIGION IN CLASSICAL SOCIOLOGY

Durkheim, Marx, and Weber had very complex and developed theories about the nature and effects of religion. Durkheim and Weber specifically are often difficult to understand, especially in light of the lack of context and examples in their primary texts. To summarize their theories, especially in brief form, is a dubious enterprise. Any attempts should be tempered by a direct reading of their works or at least reference to other texts which interpret and summarize them. It is with this warning that a summary is provided. However, religion was considered to be an extremely important social variable in the work of all three:

Karl Marx

It may be best to initially discard some common misconceptions about Marx's ideas. First of all, Marx did not view his work as an ethical or ideological response to nineteenth–century capitalism (as most later commentators have). His efforts were, in his mind, based solely on what can be called applied science. Marx saw himself as doing morally neutral sociology and economic theory for the sake of human development. As Christiano states, "Marx did not believe in science for science's sake he believed that he was also advancing a theory that would be a useful tool [in] effecting a revolutionary upheaval of the capitalist system in favor of socialism." (124) As such, the crux of his arguments was the belief that humans are best guided by reason. Religion, Marx held, was a significant hindrance to reason, inherently masking the truth and misguiding followers.

As we will later see, Marx viewed social alienation as the heart of social inequality. The antithesis to this alienation is freedom. Subsequently, to propagate freedom means to present individuals with the truth and give them a choice as to whether or not to accept or deny it. In this, "Marx never suggested that religion ought to be prohibited." (Christiano 126) But what led Marx to believe these things?

Central to his theories was the oppressive economic situation in which he dwelt. With the rise of European industrialism, Marx and his colleague Engels witnessed and responded to the growth of what he called "surplus value." Marx's view of capitalism saw rich capitalists getting richer and their workers getting poorer (the gap, the exploitation, was the "surplus value").

And not only were workers getting exploited, but in the process they were being further detached from the products they helped create. By simply selling their work for wages, "workers simultaneously lose connection with the object of labor and become objects themselves. Workers are devalued to the level of a commodity – a thing " (Ibid 125) From this objectification comes alienation. The common worker is told he or she is a replaceable tool, alienated to the point of extreme discontent. Here, in Marx's eyes, religion enters.

As an "opiate of the people," Marx recognized that religion served a true function in society – but did not agree with the foundation of that function. As Marx commentator Norman Birnbaum stated, to Marx, "religion [was] a spiritual response to a condition of alienation." (Ibid 126) Responding to alienation, Marx thought that religion served to uphold the ideologies and cultural systems that foster oppressive capitalism. Thus, "Religion was conceived to be a powerful conservative force that served to perpetuate the domination of one social class at the expense of others." (Ibid 127).

In other words, religion held together the system that oppressed lower–class individuals. And so, in Marx's infamous words, "To abolish religion as the illusory happiness of the people is to demand their real happiness. The demand to give up illusions about the existing state of affairs to the demand to give up a state of affairs which needs illusions. The criticism of religion is therefore in embryo the criticism of the vale of tears, the halo of which is religion."

Emile Durkheim

Emile Durkheim placed himself in the positivist tradition, meaning that he thought of his study of society as dispassionate and scientific. He was deeply interested in the problem of what held complex modern societies together. Religion, he argued, was an expression of social cohesion.

In the fieldwork that led to his famous Elementary Forms of Religious Life, Durkheim, who was a highly rational, secular Frenchman himself, spent fifteen years studying what he considered to be "primitive" religion among the Australian aborigines. His underlying interest was to understand the basic forms of religious life for all societies. In Elementary Forms, Durkheim makes the argument that the totemic gods the aborigines worship are actually expressions of their own conceptions of society itself. This is true not only for the aborigines, he argues, but for all societies.

Religion, for Durkheim, is not "imaginary," although he does strip it of what many believers find essential. Religion is very real; it is an expression of society itself, and indeed, there is no society that does not have religion. (That would not be possible for Durkheim.) We perceive as individuals a force greater than ourselves, which is our social life, and give that perception a supernatural face. We then express ourselves religiously in groups, which for Durkheim makes the symbolic power greater. Religion is an expression of our collective consciousness, which is the fusion of all of our individual consciousnesses, which then creates a reality of its own.

It follows, then, that less complex societies, such as the Australian aborigines, have less complex religious systems, involving totems associated with particular clans. The more complex the society, the more complex the religious system. As societies come in contact with other societies, there is a tendency for religious systems to emphasize universalism to a greater and greater extent. However, as the division of labor makes the individual seem more important (a subject that Durkheim treats extensively in his famous Division of Labor in Society), religious systems increasingly focus on individual salvation and conscience.

Durkheim's definition of religion, from Elementary Forms, is as follows: "A religion is a unified system of beliefs and practices relative to sacred things, that is to say, things set apart and forbidden – beliefs and practices which unite into one single moral community called a Church, all those who adhere to them."

This is a functional definition of religion, meaning that it explains what religion *does* in social life: essentially, it unites societies.

This definition also does not stipulate what exactly may be considered sacred. Thus, later sociologists of religion (notably Robert Bellah) have extended Durkheimian insights to talk about notions of civil religion, or the religion of a state. American civil religion, for example, might be said to have its own set of sacred "things": American flags, Abraham Lincoln, Martin Luther King, etc. Other sociologists have taken Durkheim in the direction of the religion of professional sports, or of rock music.

Max Weber

Max Weber differed from Karl Marx and Emile Durkheim in that he focused his work on the effects of religious action and inaction.

Instead of discussing religion as a kind of misapprehension (an "opiate of the people,") or as social cohesion, Weber did not attempt to reduce religion to its essence. Instead, he examines how religious ideas and groups interacted with other aspects of social life (notably the economy). In doing so, Weber often attempts to get at religion's subjective meaning to the individual.

In Weber's sociology, he uses the German term "Verstehen" to describe his method of interpretation of the intention and context of human action. Weber is not a positivist -- meaning he does not believe we can find out "facts" in sociology that are easily causally linked. Although he believes some generalized statements about social life can be made, he is not interested in hard positivist claims, but instead in linkages and sequences, in historical narratives and particular cases.

Weber argues for making sense of religious action on its own terms. A religious group or individual is influenced by all kinds of things, he says—but if they claim to be acting in the name of religion, we should attempt to understand their perspective on religious grounds first. Weber gives religion credit for shaping a person's image of the world, and this image of the world can affect their view of their interests, and ultimately how they decide to take action.

For Weber, religion is best understood as it responds to the human need for theodicy and soteriology. Human beings are troubled, he says, with the question of theodicy -- the question of how the extraordinary power of a divine god may be reconciled with the imperfection of the world that he has created and rules over. People need to know, for example, why there is undeserved good fortune and suffering in the world. Religion offers people soteriological answers, or answers that provide opportunities for salvation -- relief from suffering, and reassuring meaning. The pursuit of salvation, like the pursuit of wealth, becomes a part of human motivation.

Because religion helps to define motivation, Weber believed that religion (and specifically Protestant Calvinism) actually helped to give rise to modern capitalism, as he asserted in his most famous and controversial work, The Protestant Ethic and the Spirit of Modern Capitalism.

In Protestant Ethic, Weber argues that capitalism arose in the West in part because of how the belief in predestination was interpreted by everyday English Puritans. Puritan theology was based on the Calvinist notion that not everyone would be saved; there was only a specific number of the elect who would avoid damnation, and this was based sheerly on God's predetermined will and not on any action you could perform in this life. Official doctrine held that one could not ever really know whether one was among the elect.

Practically, Weber noted, this was difficult psychologically: people were (understandably) anxious to know whether they would be eternally damned or not. Thus Puritan leaders began assuring members that if they began doing well financially in their businesses, this would be one unofficial sign they had God's approvial and were among the saved -- but only if they used the fruits of their labor well. This led to the development of rational bookkeeping and the calculated pursuit of financial success beyond what one needed simply to live—and this is the "spirit of capitalism." Over time, the habits associated with the spirit of capitalism lost their religious significance, and rational pursuit of profit became its own aim.

The Protestant Ethic thesis has been much critiqued, refined, and disputed, but is still a lively source of theroetical debate in sociology of religion. Weber also did considerable work on world religions, including Hinduism and Buddhism.

CONTEMPORARY SOCIOLOGY OF RELIGION

Rodney Stark

According to the theory of R. Stark & W. S. Bainbridge, religions are systems of "compensators". Compensators are a body of language and practices that compensate for some physical lack or frustrated goal. They can be divided into specific compensators (compensators for the failure to achieve specific goals), and general compensators (compensators for failure to achieve any goal).

It has been observed that social or political movements that fail to achieve their goals will often transform into religions. As it becomes clear that the goals of the movement will not be achieved by natural means (at least within their lifetimes), members of the movement will look to the supernatural to achieve what cannot be achieved naturally. The new religious beliefs are compensators for the failure to achieve the original goals.

Examples of this include the counterculture movement in America: the early counterculture movement was intent on changing society and removing its injustice and boredom; but as members of the movement proved unable to achieve these goals they turned to Eastern and new religions as compensators.

A general sociological theory of the formation of religions is contained in R. Stark & W. S. Bainbridge's book "Theory of Religion". This theory is outlined roughly below:

Most religions start out their lives as cults or sects, i.e. groups in high tension with the surrounding society. Over time, they tend to either die out, or become more established, mainstream and in less tension with society.

Cults are new groups with a new novel theology, while sects are attempts to return mainstream religions to (what the sect views as) their original purity. Mainstream established groups are called denominations. The comments below about cult formation apply equally well to sect formation.

There are four models of cult formation: the Psychopathological Model, the Entrepreneurial Model, the Social Model and the Normal Revelations model.

According to the "Psychopathological Model", religions are founded during a period of severe stress in the life of the founder. The founder suffers from psychological problems, which they resolve through the founding of the religion. (The development of the religion is for them a form of self-therapy, or self-medication.)

According to the Entrepreneurial Model, founders of religions act like entrepreneurs, developing new products (religions) to sell to consumers (to convert people to). According to this model, most founders of new religions already have experience in several religious groups before they begin their own. They take ideas from the pre-existing religions, and try to improve on them to make them more popular.

The Social Model emphasises not the founder of the religion, but rather the early religious group. According to this model, religions are founded by means of social implosions. Members of the religious group spend less and less time with people outside the group, and more and more time with each other within it. The level of affection and emotional bonding between members of a group increases, and their emotional bonds to members outside the group diminish. According to the social model, when a social implosion occurs, the group will naturally develop a new theology and rituals to accompany it.

The Normal Revelations model was added to the theory by Stark in a later work. According to the Normal Revelations model, religions are founded when the founder interprets ordinary natural phenomena as supernatural; for instance, ascribing his or her own creativity in inventing the religion to that of the deity.

Some religions are better described by one model than another, though all apply to differing degrees to all religions.

Once a cult or sect has been founded, the next problem for the founder is to convert new members to it. Prime candidates for religious conversion are those with an openness to religion, but who do not belong or fit well in any existing religious group.

Those with no religion or no interest in religion are difficult to convert, especially since the cult and sect beliefs are so extreme by the standards of the surrounding society. But those already happy members of a religious group are difficult to convert as well, since they have strong social links to their pre-existing religion and are unlikely to want to sever them in order to join a new one. The best candidates for religious conversion are those who are members of or have been associated with religious groups (thereby showing an interest or openness to religion), yet exist on the fringe of these groups, without strong social ties to prevent them from joining a new group.

Potential converts vary in their level of social connection. New religions best spread through pre-existing friendship networks. Converts who are marginal with few friends are easy to convert, but having few friends to convert they cannot add much to the further growth of the organization. Converts with a large social network are harder to convert, since they tend to have more invested in mainstream society; but once converted they yield many new followers through their friendship network.

Cults initially can have quite high growth rates; but as the social networks that initially feed them are exhausted, their growth rate falls quickly. On the other hand, the rate of growth is exponential (ignoring the limited supply of potential converts): the more converts you have, the more missionaries you can have out looking for new converts.

But nonetheless it can take a very long time for religions to grow to a large size by natural growth. This often leads to cult leaders giving up after several decades, and withdrawing the cult from the world.

It is difficult for cults and sects to maintain their initial enthusiasm for more than about a generation. As children are born into the cult or sect, members begin to demand a more stable life. When this happens, cults tend to lose or de-emphasise many of their more radical beliefs, and become more open to the surrounding society; they then become denominations.

The goal or dream of most founders of religions is to convert their entire society; but of the myriad religions founded throughout history, few have been very successful. Most of the world's religious people adhere to one of a few major religions (Christianity, Islam, Hinduism, Buddhism, Judaism). It is very difficult for a religion to grow to this size. Most of these religions (especially Christianity) became established when they were adopted by politically powerful individuals. The religion of the common people took much longer to change (sometimes centuries).

4

SOCIOLOGY OF SCIENCE AND TECHNOLOGY

SOCIOLOGY OF SCIENCE AND TECHNOLOGY

The *sociology of science and technology* is a broad field combining elements of the rich interdisciplinary field of science studies, as well as distinct sociological theories on the history of science.

Science Studies

Science studies is an interdisciplinary research area that seeks to situate scientific expertise in a broad social, historical, and philosophical context. It is concerned with the history of scientific disciplines, the interrelationships between science and society, and the alleged covert purposes that underlie scientific claims. While it is critical of science, it holds out the possibility of broader public participation in science policy issues.

Theories and Sociology of the History of Science

The sociology and philosophy of science, as well as the entire field of science studies, have in the 20th century been preoccupied with the question of large-scale patterns and trends in the development of science, and asking questions about how science "works" both in a philosophical and practical sense.

ESTABLISHING THE FIELD OF HUMAN ECOLOGY

In the USA, human ecology was established as a sociological field in the late 1970s by William R. Catton and Riley E. Dunlap, building onto the earlier works on human ecology by Chicago School's Robert E. Park. One main idea of Catton and Dunlap was to go away from the Durkheimian paradigm of explaining social facts only with social facts. Instead, they included physical and biological facts as independent variables influencing social structure and other social phenomenons.

This change of paradigm can be described as a change from a classical sociological view of *human exemptionalism* to a new view (named *new ecological paradigm* by Catton and Dunlap). Humans are no longer the exeptional species that can use culture to adapt onto new environments and environmental change, and that is influenced more by social than by biological variables, but they are seen as one species out of many that interacts with a bounded natural environment.

A conflict line between this new paradigm and the classical sociological approach is the de-valuating of society and culture. Human ecology views human communities and human populations as part of the ecosystem of earth. In this view, sociology would be only a sub-discipline of ecology—the special ecology of the species *homo sapiens sapiens*. Of course, this is seen as an affront by most sociologists.

It is disputed if human ecology is a sub-discipline of sociology, or if it is a sub-discipline of ecology. A point that strengthens the latter position is the methodological approach of human ecology, that is orientation rather along the lines of natural science then along the lines of social sciences. The inclusion or exclusion of human ecology in to sociology proper varies between countries and schools of sociological thinking. Environmental sociology is a field of sociology which encompasses the interactions between humans and nature/natural environment, but is rooted in the methodological and theoretical canon of sociology. Sometimes human ecology is seen as part of environmental sociology, sometimes it is seen as something completly different. Influences can also be seen between human ecology and the field of political ecology.

Quotes on Human Ecology

Human Ecology is an interdisciplinary applied field that uses a holistic approach to help people solve problems and enhance human potential within their near environments - their clothing, family, home, and community. Human Ecologists promote the well-being of individuals, families, and communities through education, prevention, and empowerment.

Human ecology explores not only the influence of humans on their environment but also the influence of the environment on human behaviour, and their adaptive strategies as they come to understand those influences better. [...] For us, human ecology is a methodology as much as an area of research. It is a way of thinking about the world, and a context in which we define our questions and ways to answer those questions.

Industrial Sociology (Sociology of Work) is the study of the interaction of people in the workplace. It includes the study of boss-subordinate, inter-departmental, and management / trade-union relationships.

Industrial and organizational psychology (or **I/O psychology**) is the study of the behavior of people in the workplace. Industrial and organizational psychology attempts to apply psychological results and methods to aid workers and organizations. It is also known as **occupational psychology** (the commonest name in the United Kingdom and **work psychology** (the direct translation of the standard term in German, *Arbeitpsychologie*).

Industrial and organizational psychologists use psychological tests and assessments to measure the knowledge, skills, abilities, and other characteristics (KSAOs) of people for a variety of employment-related purposes, such as selection for hiring or promotion, training and development, or measuring employee satisfaction. Historically, the job analysis has been the traditional means by which the essential KSAOs associated with any particular position are identified.

It is a fairly diverse field incorporating aspects of fields such as clinical psychology, social psychology, and psychometrics as well as broader social studies such as organizational theory, law, and gender issues.

Related Disciplines

industrial engineering

quality management

psychometrics

social psychology

labor and industrial relations

organizational development

Many industrial and organizational psychologists specialize in "I" aspects (e.g., psychometrics; time and motion studies; labor law) or "O" aspects (e.g., leadership selection, coaching and development; organizational design and change). Some I/O psychologists are academic or non-academic researchers while many others are engaged in practice, holding positions such as:

executive coach

diversity consultant

legislative compliance officer

labor relations specialist

human resources specialist

process improvement consultant

manager of selection and training.

Medical sociology is the study of individual and group behaviors with respect to health and illness. In this regard, "medical" is a bit of a misnomer, because the focus is not on medical professionals or their behaviors, but on human behavioral responses to health and illness, which overlaps with the domain of nursing more than that of medicine. (See 1995 American Nurses Association: Nursing's Social Policy Statement.) Medical sociology is concerned with individual and group responses directed toward assessing well-being, maintaining health, acting upon illness (whether real or perceived), interacting with health care systems, and maximizing health in the face of physiologic or functional derangement. Along with analyzing the ways in which our health is a result of the psychological conditons as a result of our environment.

Political Sociology is the study of sociology within the area of Politics. This area of sociology is widely related to geopolitics.

RURAL SOCIOLOGY

Rural sociology is a field of sociology associated with the study of life in small towns and the country. It is a scientific study of social arrangements and behaviour amongst peoples that are distanced from points of concentrated activity. Much of rural sociology involves the examination of statistical data.

Agribusiness is the predominant focus of rural sociology and much of this field is dedicated to the economics of farm production.

Definition of Rural

Sociologists define **rural** as those areas which are not urban. Rural sociology, then, contrasts with urban sociology. Urban areas are usually defined in terms of size and population density. The line between urban and rural is quite arbitrary. However, rural settlement patterns tend to be, relatively, small in scale and low in density.

In the US, a rural region is one with fewer than 2,500 people. In Japan, a rural region is one with fewer than 50,000 people. Meanwhile, some places with 1,000 people seem quite urbanized while other places with 15,000 people seem quite rural. Also, many "rural" areas are adjacent to very large metropolises. 1995, there were 2,288 rural counties in the US, constituting 83% of the land and home to 21% (51,000,000) of the population.

Rural Economic Trends

Net cash farm income was projected at US$ 53.7 billion for 1999.

Currently, rural capital is flowing into either urban areas or some 33-40% of rural counties, namely the intermountain West, the Ozarks, counties along I-80 in Nebraska, and the Kansas City area. The growth of wealth is concentrated near urban areas, transportation corridors, and scenic amenities.

Rural America is also experiencing an economic slump, for instant in 1999 the prices for sweetcorn, wheat, and soybeans were all down about 33% from the 1995-1998 average. Food production is being subsidized by off-farm income. Working second and third jobs is the only way many farmers can survive. In 1974, 80% of farm operators were primarily farmers, by 1997 that had dropped to 60%.

Natural resource-based industries, within rural areas, are experiencing resource depletion. The economic importance of mining, light manufacturing, and agriculture are considered to be on the decline, within these areas.

Issues in Rural America

Rural society is faced with various problems including the environmental degradation and overuse of water resources, the establishment and inadequate regulation of toxic waste dumps, and poverty. The loss of rural population to urban areas is also an area of concern, especially in northern states, such as North Dakota.

Fred Buttel asks, "Will we witness a further erosion of commitment to improving the livelihoods of the rural poor?"

History of Rural Sociology

Rural sociology became prominent, during the late industrial revolution, in France, Ireland, Prussia, Scandinavia, and the US. As urban incomes and quality of life rose, a social gap appeared between urban and rural dwellers.

In the 1920s, Edmund deS. Brunner studied some 140 villages as director of the Institute for Social and Religious Research, he reported that as agriculture mechanized, farms were growing larger.

After World War II, modern rural sociology began to appear in France, Germany, Italy, the Netherlands, and the UK.

Key Topics in Rural Sociology

agribusiness

role homogeneity

rural exodus

types of rural communities.

AGRIBUSINESS

Agribusiness is a term that describes the corporate method of farming. The term includes not only the farm itself but also the entire chain of agriculture-related business including seed supply, food processing, machinery, etc. Agribusiness marks the rise of modern techno-farming. Farms are expensive to operate; costs include machinery, fertilizers, pesticides, fuel, and seeds. Some people question whether small family farms are economically sustainable in the United States. One major difference between independent farming and corporate farming is that a corporate farmer is usually a contracted employee, rather than the "boss" of the farm.

The goal of agribusiness is to vertically integrate all food production. Corporations want to manage every step of this production, from DNA to consumption. One of the biggest agribusinesses is Archer Daniels Midland.

HISTORY OF AGRIBUSINESS

The corporate farming movement began in the chicken and vegetable industries and has since expanded to hog and grain production. In 1997, some 60% of hogs sold within the US were sold under some form of contract, whereas in 1980 only 5% of hogs were sold in this manner.

Criticism of Agribusiness

Agribusiness has received criticism because of its tendency to remove farmers from independent production decisions and forcing them to sign production contracts with corporations. Agribusiness is also criticized for its tendency to concentrate production, while expanding, and thus steadily decrease both the number of farms and the percentage of independent farmers. This is essentially an anti-monopolist criticism.

As production continues to concentrate and is coupled with increasing reliance on technology, farmers complain about their increasing remoteness from centers of population or production. Fox example, farm machinery repair services, which were once as close as 2 miles away, are increasingly as far as 40 miles away.

Robert A. Rohwer asks, "Are we starting a new serfdom with CEOs as the lords? Are we creating a vise whose jaws are corporate control? Corporations will soon collect all the windfalls of agriculture and corporate decisions will dominate all aspects of the field. My son and daughter are mere employees, tied to the land, swamped in debt, and diminished in their entrepreneurship. We are moving towards industrialized agriculture."

It is important to consider whether the food that reaches the consumer is as good as it would be under alternative structures of the food industry. Very large organisations may be motivated primarily to maximise yield and profit rather than breadth of choice (to the consumer) and flavour; they may feel more inclined to use genetically modified crops, hormones, preservatives, color additives and insectides to maximise yield and profit.

In the United Kingdom there has been a growing reaction against factory farmed produce in recent years, with consumers feeling that they can obtain higher quality products (admittedly at a higher price) if they know the provenance (the local and often small scale source) of the food they buy. There is little or no comparative information about flavours compared internationally and over time (i.e today compared with the past) but there is anecdotal evidence that US factory farming may have resulted in a deterioration (and not simply a change) of food flavours.

In sociology, **role homogeneity** is the degree of overlap amongst the different roles performed by different members of a community.

Role Homogeneity and Rural Sociology

Rural sociologists often note that amongst rural communities there exists a very high degree of role homogeneity, that is, one person may perform the duties of banker, coach, deacon, school board member, and neighbor.

Role Homogeneity and Controversy

Sociologists have demonstrated that in areas of strong homogeneity, there is a general tendency to repress controversy. As a result, when disagreements arise, they can result into serious crises. Such communities tend to have local newspapers which are more orientated towards marketing, rather than news. What news is published, in a highly-homogeneous society, tends to focus on non-controversial topics and avoid "bad news".

RURAL EXODUS

Rural Exodus is a term used to describe the migratory patterns that normally occur in a region following the mechanisation of agriculture. In such a situation, there tends to be a movement of peoples from rural areas into urban areas. This trend can be particularly disruptive and enfeebling to rural life if the out-migrants tend to be younger adults, which are viewed as if they were an invested resource.

The term **rural exodus states** is used to refer to those US states which are losing their rural populations in this manner. These states tend to be within the Great Plains and have few scenic amenities, along with harsh summers and severe winters.

URBAN EXODUS

In recent years *"urban exodus"* has also been portrayed as a problem with migrants from towns being seen as unwilling to socialise, having unrealistic expectations of local services (eg.medical and transport facilities) and a cause of accelerating property values to the detriment of potential occupiers born in the locality with lower borrowing and spending power.

Sociologists have identified a number of different **types of rural communities**, which have arisen as a result of changing economic trends within rural regions of industrial nations.

The basic trend seems to be one in which communities are required to become entrepreneurial. Those that lack the sort of characteristics mentioned below, are forced to either seek out their niche or accept eventual economic defeat.

These towns focus on marketing and public relations whilst bidding for business and government operations; such as, off-site data processing or, perhaps, a factory.

For instance; International Falls, Minnesota markets itself as a site for sub-zero temperature experiments; Ottawa, Illinois managed to attract three Japanese firms; Freeport, Maine has become a center for mail-order companies such as L.L. Bean; and Mobile, Arizona has become the home of a number of solid-waste landfills.

Academic Communities

Academic communities are those in which the primary employers are boarding schools, colleges, universities, research laboratories, and corporate training facilities. These communities bring people away from other regions and thus bring new capital into the area.

Academic institutions, in rural areas, are very much like a factory in that the economic success of the community depends upon the success of the institution. Unlike factories, academic institutions tend to primarily offer jobs in the medium-skilled to professional range.

Examples: Ames, Iowa; Bath, Maine; Madison, Wisconsin; Plainfield, Vermont;

Area Trade-Centers

The automobile allows rural residents to travel farther, in less time, for goods and services. This reduces the importance of the rural store, along with decreasing rural population (see: rural exodus). As business relocate from impoverished communities, one town will become the trade center for it's region, sometimes doing so by constructing a mall.

Generally, business in a trade-center town, except for thos in competition with the mall, will benefit from the mall's prescence as shoppers spill over. These trade centers will knock out businesses in, and thus impoverish, nearby towns as shoppers converge on the town with the greatest variety of stores.

Government Centers

Rural regions are undergoing increasing government consolidation. This results in a small number of towns becoming centers of government activity, while the rest are devoid of government infrastructure. These centers include state and local capitals, and areas with prisons or military bases.

Centralized public administration focuses public-sector employment on a single community, assisting it over its neighbors. Benefits, for the government center, include improved public services, increased efficiency, and economic savings.

Recreation Communities

Recreation communities (tourist towns) define some local feature, usually a historic site or scenic vista, as a "natural resource" and market this to tourists. Travelers will then spend money on food, hotels, and the like, which brings capital into the town.

See: Deadwood, South Dakota; Harper's Ferry, West Virginia;; Tombstone, Arizona; St. Charles, Missouri; Pleasant Hill, Kentucky; Intercourse, Pennsylvania

Retirement Communities

Retirement communities tend to house large numbers of elderly people. These retirees, bring pensions, Social

Security, and savings which infuse the area with capital. Rural hospitals are increasingly unable to bring enough patients to support their operational budget, and retirement communities have developed, in some areas, as a means to solve this problem.

It should be noted that elderly residents, who migrate from the cities, tend to have above average wealth, thus creating an income disparity between the migrant retirees and the local elderly.

TYPOLOGY

Social scientists tend to assume no supernatural intervention in the formation of religions, viewing them in the same way they view the development of other social structures.

Typology of Religious Groups

According to what is at present the most common typology among sociologists, religious groups are classified as ecclesia, denominations, cults or sects. Note that sociologists give these words precise definitions which are different from how they are commonly used. Note especially that the words 'cult' and 'sect' as used by sociologists are free from prejudice, even though the popular use of these words is often highly pejorative.

THE SOCIOLOGICAL VIEW OF RELIGION

The below text deals only with one theory; work of other authors needs to be included.

According to the theory of R. Stark & W. S. Bainbridge, religions are systems of "compensators". Compensators are a body of language and practices that compensate for some physical lack or frustrated goal. They can be divided into specific compensators (compensators for the failure to achieve specific goals), and general compensators (compensators for failure to achieve any goal).

It has been observed that social or political movements that fail to achieve their goals will often transform into religions. As it becomes clear that the goals of the movement will not be achieved by natural means (at least within their lifetimes), members of the movement will look to the supernatural to achieve what cannot be achieved naturally. The new religious beliefs are compensators for the failure to achieve the original goals.

Examples of this include the counterculture movement in America: the early counterculture movement was intent on changing society and removing its injustice and boredom; but as members of the movement proved unable to achieve these goals they turned to Eastern and new religions as compensators.

Sociological Theories of the Formation of Religion

The most general sociological theory of the formation of religions so far is contained in R. Stark & W. S. Bainbridge's book "Theory of Religion". This theory is outlined roughly below:

Most religions start out their lives as cults or sects, i.e. groups in high tension with the surrounding society. Over time, they tend to either die out, or become more established, mainstream and in less tension with society. Cults are new groups with a new novel theology, while sects are attempts to return mainstream religions to (what the sect views as) their original purity. Mainstream established groups are called denominations. The comments below about cult formation apply equally well to sect formation.

There are four models of cult formation: the Psychopathological Model, the Entrepreneurial Model, the Social Model and the Normal Revelations model.

According to the Psychopathological Model, religions are founded during a period of severe stress in the life of the founder. The founder suffers from psychological problems, which they resolve through the founding of the religion. (The development of the religion is for them a form of self-therapy, or self-medication.)

According to the Entrepreneurial Model, founders of religions act like entrepreneurs, developing new products (religions) to sell to consumers (to convert people to). According to this model, most founders of new religions already have experience in several religious groups before they begin their own. They take ideas from the pre-existing religions, and try to improve on them to make them more popular.

The Social Model emphasises not the founder of the religion, but rather the early religious group. According to this model, religions are founded by means of social implosions. Members of the religious group spend less and less time with people outside the group, and more and more time with each other within it. The level of affection and emotional bonding between members of a group increases, and their emotional bonds to members outside the group diminsh. According to the social model, when a social implosion occurs, the group will naturally develop a new theology and rituals to accompany it.

The Normal Revelations model was added to the theory by Stark in a latter work. According to the Normal Revelations model, religions are founded when the founder interprets ordinary natural phenomena as supernatural;

for instance, ascribing his or her own creativity in inventing the religion to that of the deity.

Some religions are better described by one model than another, though all apply to differing degrees to all religions.

Once a cult or sect has been founded, the next problem for the founder is to convert new members to it. Prime candidates for religious conversion are those with an openness to religion, but who do not belong or fit well in any existing religious group. Those with no religion or no interest in religion are difficult to convert, especially since the cult and sect beliefs are so extreme by the standards of the surrounding society. But those already happy members of a religious group are difficult to convert as well, since they have strong social links to their pre-existing religion and are unlikely to want to sever them in order to join a new one. The best candidates for religious conversion are those who are members of or have been associated with religious groups (thereby showing an interest or openness to religion), yet exist on the fringe of these groups, without strong social ties to prevent them from joining a new group.

Potential converts vary in their level of social connection. New religions best spread through pre-existing friendship networks. Converts who are marginal with few friends are easy to convert, but having few friends to convert they cannot add much to the further growth of the organization. Converts with a large social network are harder to convert, since they tend to have more invested in mainstream society; but once converted they yield many new followers through their friendship network.

Cults initially can have quite high growth rates; but as the social networks that initially feed them are exhausted, their growth rate falls quickly. On the other hand, the rate of growth is exponential (ignoring the limited supply of potential converts): the more converts you have, the more missionaries you can have out looking for new converts. But nonetheless it can take a very long time for religions to grow to a large size by natural growth. This often leads to cult leaders giving up after several decades, and withdrawing the cult from the world.

It is difficult for cults and sects to maintain their initial enthusiasm for more than about a generation. As children are born into the cult or sect, members begin to demand a more stable life. When this happens, cults tend to lose or de-emphasise many of their more radical beliefs, and become more open to the surrounding society; they then become denominations.

The goal or dream of most founders of religions is to convert their entire society; but of the myriad religions founded throughout history, few have been very successful. Most of the world's religious market share is taken up by a few religions (Christianity, Islam, Hinduism, Buddhism). It is very difficult for a religion to grow to this size, and depends more on the luck than the skill of the religion's founder. Most of these religions (especially Christianity) established themselves by penetrating the social network of the society's elite. Once this network was penetrated, the religion quickly controlled the elite of the society. The religion of the common people took much longer to change (sometimes centuries), but once the elite had changed their religion the change of the whole society was inevitable.

SYSTEMS THEORY

Systems theory or **general systems theory** or **systemics** is an interdisciplinary field which studies systems as a whole. Systems theory was founded by Ludwig von Bertalanffy, William Ross Ashby and others between the

1940s and the 1970s on principles from physics, biology and engineering and later grew into philosophy, sociology and economics. Cybernetics is a related field, sometimes considered as a part of systems theory.

Systems theory focuses on complexity and interdependance. It has a strong philosophical dimension, because applied to the human mind and society, it results in unusual perspectives. In recent times **complex systems** has increasingly been used as a synonym.

Part of systems theory, *system dynamics* is a method for understanding the dynamic behavior of complex systems. The basis of the method is the recognition that the structure of any system—the many circular, interlocking, sometimes time-delayed relationships among its components—is often just as important in determining its behavior as the individual components themselves. Examples are chaos theory and social dynamics.

In recent years, the field of *systems thinking* has been developed to provide techniques for studying systems in holistic ways to supplement more traditional reductionistic methods. In this more recent tradition, systems theory is considered by some as a humanistic counterpart to the natural sciences.

URBAN SOCIOLOGY

Urban sociology is the sociological study of the various statistics among the population in cities. (*See also*: Rural sociology).

There are many areas of study in urban sociology. Among them population,geopolitics, economics etc.

The Chicago School is a major influence in the study of urban sociology. Despite having studies cities in the early

20th century, the Chicago School is still recognized as important.

SOCIOLOGY OF KNOWLEDGE

The **sociology of knowledge** is the study of the social origins of ideas, and of the effects that prevailing ideas have on societies. (Compare history of ideas.)

The term first came into widespread use in the 1920s, when a number of German-speaking sociologists wrote extensively on it, notably Max Scheler, and Karl Mannheim with *Ideology and Utopia*. With the dominance of functionalism through the middle years of the 20th century, the sociology of knowledge tended to remain on the periphery of mainstream sociological thought. It was largely reinvented and applied much more closely to everyday life in the 1960s, particularly by Peter L. Berger and Thomas Luckmann in *The social construction of reality* (1966) and is still central for methods dealing with qualitative understanding of human society. Compare socially constructed reality.

Although, very influential within modern sociology, the sociology of knowledge can claim its most significant impact on science more generally through its contribution to debate and understanding of the nature of science itself, most notably through the work of Thomas Kuhn on *The structure of scientific revolutions*.

SCHOOLS

Karl Mannheim

to be written

Phenomenological Sociology

to be written

Michel Foucault

A particularly important strain of the sociology of knowledge is the criticism by Michel Foucault. In "Madness and Civilization: A History of Insanity in the Age of Reason", 1961, he argued that conceptions of madness and what was considered "reason" or "knowledge" was itself subject to major culture bias—in this respect mirroring similar criticisms by Thomas Szasz, at the time the foremost critic of psychiatry - and himself now an eminent psychiatrist. A point where Foucault and Ssasz agreed was that sociological processes played the major role in defining "madness" as an "illness" and prescribing "cures".

In "The Birth of the Clinic: An Archaeology of Medical Perception", 1963, Foucault extended his critique to all of modern scientific medicine, arguing for the central conceptual metaphor of "The Gaze", which had implications for medical education, prison design, and the carceral state as understood today. Concepts of criminal justice and its intersection with medicine were better developed in this work than in Ssasz and others who confined their critique to current psychiatric practice.

Finally, in "The Order of Things: An Archaeology of the Human Sciences", 1966, and "The Archaeology of Knowledge, 1969, Foucault introduced the abstract notions of mathesis and taxonomia. These, he claimed, had transformed 17th and 18th century studies of "general grammar" into modern "linguistics", "natural history" into modern "biology", and "analysis of wealth" into modern "economics". Not, claimed Foucault, without loss of meaning. The 19th century had transformed what knowledge was.

Perhaps Foucault's best-known and most controversial claim was that before the 18th century, "Man did not exist". The notions of humanity and of humanism were inventions or creations of this 19th century transformation. Accordingly, a cognitive bias had been introduced unwittingly into science, by over-trusting the individual doctor or scientist's ability to see and state things objectively. This study still guides sociology of knowledge and has been claimed to have sparked single-handed much of postmodernism. Foucault is taught as core curriculum to French high school students, who also study Nietzsche and his claim that "God is dead".

BRUNO LATOUR

The Sociology of Mathematical Knowledge

Studies of mathematical practice and quasi-empiricism in mathematics are also rightly part of the sociology of knowledge, since they focus on the community of those who practice mathematics and their common assumptions. Since Eugene Wigner raised the issue in 1960 and Hilary Putnam made it more rigorous in 1975, the question of why fields such as physics and mathematics should agree so well has been in question. There is simply no explanation for this, other than sociological agreement, and usefulness of mathematics to predict unobserved phenomena in physics—pure circumstance, and nothing that a mathematician would call a "proof".

George Lakoff and others who advocate a cognitive science of mathematics argue that the social interactions and disciplined practices of what is now called cognitive science are the only way to overcome the now-generally-acknowledged cognitive bias in mathematics itself, or alternately, that it cannot be overcome at all, and thus that the sociology of knowledge and its creation and editing are only applicable to the human species.

An interesting artifact in the sociology of knowledge is the Erdos number derived from the graph of all mathematicians who collaborated with Paul Erdos, thousands of them, on number theory. Serious studies of this graph have barely begun, but there appear to be collaborations sparked purely by the graph as structure in itself. Thus, the notions of sociology of knowledge, and of sacred geometry in the form of the graph itself (Erdos' feat is unlikely or impossible to repeat, certainly in any near term future), seem to be converging, with no more insight as to why mathematics works well to organize what we call "knowledge", and what Foucault called a "mathesis".

The **sociology of knowledge** is the study of the social origins of ideas, and of the effects that prevailing ideas have on societies. (Compare history of ideas.)

The term first came into widespread use in the 1920s, when a number of German-speaking sociologists wrote extensively on it, notably Max Scheler, and Karl Mannheim with *Ideology and Utopia*. With the dominance of functionalism through the middle years of the 20th century, the sociology of knowledge tended to remain on the periphery of mainstream sociological thought.

It was largely reinvented and applied much more closely to everyday life in the 1960s, particularly by Peter L. Berger and Thomas Luckmann in *The social construction of reality* (1966) and is still central for methods dealing with qualitative understanding of human society. Compare socially constructed reality.

Although, very influential within modern sociology, the sociology of knowledge can claim its most significant impact on science more generally through its contribution to debate and understanding of the nature of science itself, most notably through the work of Thomas Kuhn on *The structure of scientific revolutions*.

Schools

Karl Mannheim

to be written

Phenomenological sociology

to be written

Michel Foucault

A particularly important strain of the sociology of knowledge is the criticism by Michel Foucault. In "Madness and Civilization: A History of Insanity in the Age of Reason", 1961, he argued that conceptions of madness and what was considered "reason" or "knowledge" was itself subject to major culture bias - in this respect mirroring similar criticisms by Thomas Szasz, at the time the foremost critic of psychiatry - and himself now an eminent psychiatrist. A point where Foucault and Ssasz agreed was that sociological processes played the major role in defining "madness" as an "illness" and prescribing "cures".

In "The Birth of the Clinic: An Archaeology of Medical Perception", 1963, Foucault extended his critique to all of modern scientific medicine, arguing for the central conceptual metaphor of "The Gaze", which had implications for medical education, prison design, and the carceral state as understood today. Concepts of criminal justice and its intersection with medicine were better developed in this work than in Ssasz and others who confined their critique to current psychiatric practice.

Finally, in "The Order of Things: An Archaeology of the Human Sciences", 1966, and "The Archaeology of Knowledge, 1969, Foucault introduced the abstract notions of mathesis and taxonomia. These, he claimed, had transformed 17th and 18th century studies of "general grammar" into modern "linguistics", "natural history" into modern "biology", and "analysis of wealth" into modern "economics". Not, claimed Foucault, without loss of meaning. The 19th century had transformed what knowledge was.

Perhaps Foucault's best-known and most controversial claim was that before the 18th century, "Man did not exist". The notions of humanity and of humanism were inventions or creations of this 19th century transformation. Accordingly, a cognitive bias had been introduced unwittingly into science, by over-trusting the individual doctor or scientist's ability to see and state things objectively. This study still guides sociology of knowledge and has been claimed to have sparked single-handed much of postmodernism. Foucault is taught as core curriculum to French high school students, who also study Nietzsche and his claim that "God is dead".

STRUCURALISM

The term ***structuralism*** is used in many contexts in different disciplines in the 20th century. Structuralism proposes the idea that many phenomena do not occur in isolation, but instead occur in relation to each other, and that all related phenomena are part of a whole with a definite, but not necessarily defined, structure. Structuralists, in any area of knowledge, attempt to perceive that structure and the changes that it may undergo with the goal of furthering the development of that system of phenomena or ideas.

In film and literary theory and criticism, the term refers to a line of thought stemming from the structural linguistics usually identified with Ferdinand de Saussure. The generalization of linguistic models by the French anthropologist Claude Levi-Strauss inspired others to apply their versions of structuralist ideas to a wide range of subjects. Thus, Levi-Strauss' views affected the social sciences from the 1960s and onward.

As with any cultural movement, the influences and developments are complex; other linguists besides Saussure were important. Roman Jakobson, in particular, worked on specifically literary problems long before structuralism became a general trend. For a description of structuralist principles, Levi-Strauss is an adequate representative of the approach; trained in both philosophy and social science, he states his views methodically.

Also, other major figures in structuralism have written a good deal of work in which other influences dominate. Both Roland Barthes and Michel Foucault have been called both structuralists and post-structuralists. Louis Althusser's chief concern was to enlarge Marxist theory. In America, the work of Leonard Bloomfield, who was inspired by Saussure, represents a more specific sense of structuralism, which is now thought to be too restrictive. In the fifties, Noam Chomsky rigorously criticized many aspects of structuralism, while at the same time he contributed to it as it is perceived today.

But Levi-Strauss was an anthropologist, a point to remember in searches for further information. He uses certain terms, including "structuralism," in the way his field uses them, even though they have other meanings elsewhere. He repeatedly contrasts structural anthropology with the work of "functionalists" while relying on two linguistic authorities, Roman Jakobson and Nicolas Troubetzkoy, who are functionalists as far as many linguists are concerned. Indeed, the purpose of calling them functionalists, along with other members of the Prague School, is to distinguish their work from the structural linguistics of Saussure. Even more confusingly, the Prague

School is occasionally referred to as "functional-structuralist", while there is a well-known position in the social sciences, deriving from Talcott Parsons, which is sometimes called "structural functionalism." A Google search on any of these terms can be exasperating.)

Structuralism in Linguistics

Structural linguists make the influential argument that the elements of a language have no intrinsic character. They take on a character only in relation to each other.

For example, human beings can make a certain range of noises, but the sound of "m" is not really the sound of "m" outside of a language that uses an "m." Within that language, a certain range of noises gets classified together as equivalent versions of the "m" sound, and there is no useful way to describe this classification except by referring to the language. The boundaries are imprecise--people who hear an "m" are not measuring waveforms and rejecting the ones beyond a certain cutoff point. Furthermore, there is change through time, local variation, and a good deal of overlap between the range of noises that can be classified as "m" and those that can be classified as something else. If there is an "m" sound that exists in the language, it must be thought of as something persisting through the welter of possible variations.

The phoneme has some essential character, apart from all its manifestations. Furthermore, the language defines this essential character partly by differentiating it from other phonemes. What makes an "m" is partly its distinction from "n." But what makes an "n" is partly its distinction from "m."

Continuing this line of analysis, it must be the case that the ?m? sound in one language is not the same a : the ?m?

sound in another, even if the same range of vocal noise is classified as ?m? in each. The classification is being made by contrasts within two different systems.

Saussure believed that the meanings expressed in a language were determined by an analogous system of differences.

This way of thinking has several obvious characteristics. It defines the boundaries of a language by reference to its internal structure.

It portrays the workings of a language solely in terms of the internal structure, rather than seeking a set of causes, functions, or patterns that could underlie several different structures. If generalized from phonetics to meaning, the approach obviously raises the possibility that what's expressed in one language cannot be expressed in any other.

Most pervasively, it depends on a notion of purely abstract structure underlying all the particular manifestations of a language. Language is not the sound, it is the classification of sounds; it is not the question, it is the comparison with other sentence types that define what a question is; it is not the idea, it is the set of underlying distinctions that make the idea possible.

This idealism, if that is the term, has a somewhat surprising result. Sign and meaning tend to merge. A word means just what it means in the language that uses it, and only that word expresses it. So, implicitly, languages are not translatable into each other. This is a possibility taken up by deconstructionism.

Structuralism in Psychology

In psychology, structuralism refers mainly to the work of Wilhelm Wundt and Edward B. Titchener, who investigated the mind by directing subjects to introspect and recording the subjects' reports.

Structuralism in General Human Culture

Levi-Strauss extends this form of linguistic analysis to all human culture. But he assumes that there is a knowable structure underlying all actions. All the operations of human consciousness and action are built on simple contrasts-the raw and the cooked, the wet and the dry, and so forth. In his view, these contrasts are changeless and universal.

In this respect, he is extending another aspect of linguistic research, the search for a universal grammar. Cultures cannot be explained without some reference to universals, located in a fundamental structure of the human mind, which must necessarily be expressed in every human act.

One implication of this view is that the same structures will operate in both the actions being studied and the scholar's interpretation of them. Freud may completely misread a folktale's meaning, in the sense of giving a bad description of the psychological tensions that its tellers had in them to express. But his response to the tale nevertheless arises from the same basis as theirs. It is at least relevant to a good description of what the tale means. Levi-Strauss explored this sort of ambiguity in his later MYTHOLOGIES.

Now, a brief illustration of structuralist analysis. In 1977, Levi-Strauss recorded an informal series of talks for the Canadian Broadcasting Corporation, presenting his views in layman's terms. The talks were published in 1979 as MYTH AND MEANING. At one point, Levi-Strauss commented on the puzzling recurrence of a musical theme in Wagner's *Ring Cycle*. The analysis is a good example because it is quick and entirely verbal (where thorough structural presentation often requires charts and tables and ad hoc borrowings of algebraic notation).

In the Rheingold, the character Alberich renounces all human love in order to receive a treasure of gold, and the theme is played. Later his wealth allows him to seduce a woman who later bears his son.

The theme is played again in the Valkyrie at a puzzling moment. Siegmund embarks on an incestuous relationship with his sister, after extracting a sword that is embedded in a tree. The scene is unlike the first one--instead of renouncing love, a man is embarking on it. His sister will later give birth to Siegfried.

The music plays again later in the Valkyrie as the king of the gods consigns his daughter Brunhilde to an enchanted sleep in a ring of fire.

What Levi-Strauss notices is that in each scene there is a protected or obstructed treasure-- the gold at the bottom of the Rhine, the sword held in a tree, the woman held in a ring of fire. The repetition of the music responds to this similarity.

In fact, says Levi-Strauss, the three objects merge. The gold is a way to a position of power which eventuates in a son, the extraction of the sword opens the way to a sexual conquest that also produces a son, and each of the sons will eventually possess Brunhilde, the woman in the fire. And she, of all the characters in this multi-generational story, will in the end return the gold to the river.

Thus, by considering a structural element common to three situations, Levi-Strauss finds a sense in which the situations are related, outside the cause-and-effect of plot. This analysis has two properties characteristic of structuralism. The structuralist comparison runs somewhat at odds with the plot sense of the scenes--the same music occurs at a moment of renunciation and a moment of love. And the analysis allows a certain shifting of use or meaning among the analogous elements. The gold and the sword are buried treasures that become instruments of conquest, while the woman is more like the object of conquest, and the music is linked to her in a scene where she the treasure is being confined rather than extracted. She returns the gold to the Rhine partly because she is identified with it, but in this action the nature of the identification becomes ambiguous--does she return the gold, or is the gold acting through her?

Now, these meanings are simple, used only to illustrate method. An opera lover might perceive them (or correct them) without any set critical approach.

Where structuralism becomes useful is in organizing large bodies of material, such as the kinship systems that Levi-Strauss initially studied or the mythologies that occupied him later. Applied to criticism, it takes the form of considering many texts, many films.

Outlook

To be blunt, this approach strains the abilities of many writers. It requires a meticulous examination of the material, and its ambition is to find the patterns that underlie just about everything. So its use as a general outlook on art and society is somewhat questionable, compared to the influential work it has produced in specialized fields. In Hellenistic studies, for example, the understanding of the myths and rites of sacrifice requires a grasp of the basic oppositions that generate all Hellenistic ideas of sacrifice: god vs. man, animal vs. man, heaven vs. earth. But one must also understand how the myrrh tree, which produces a perfume used in some rites, is defined in an entire body of knowledge about plants. Myrrh was also used as a sexual perfume, so the relation of the plant world to marriage customs is part of the same story.

For the essayist at large, structuralist methods can blend easily into the practice of attending only to the facts that support a preconception. The persistent criticism of structuralist work has been just that. Historical influences, local meanings, plot structure and other conscious work--in a word, context--provide one way of interpreting the details of a text. When structural analysis is not carried through methodically, specific interpretations can be dismissed with nothing to replace them but arbitrary claims.

Several aspects of structuralism open the way for the revision known as deconstruction. As mentioned, the Saussurean linguistic theory strongly implies that meanings cannot be translated. If the original author and the commentator are playing variations on the same structure whether the interpretation can be judged right or not, then variations may be seen as having value in themselves. And if the Western tradition of historical and critical thinking only exists within a framework of continuing mythical thought, then attention may turn to exposing how this framework is concealed.

SOCIAL CLASS

A **social class** is a group of people that have similar social and economic status.

The most common class division has either been bi-partite or tri-partite: a ruling class or "nobility" as the Upper Class and one or two lower strata. Ancient England and other European countries had a nobility and a peasantry, but gradually a Middle Class arose.

With the material prosperity stemming from the Industrial Revolution, most Western countries settled into three strata:

an Upper Class of the immensely wealthy and/or powerful

a Middle Class of professional and other workers

a Lower Class

The composition and characteristics of the Lower Class, especially in the United States, is highly controversial; some writers eschew the term *Lower Class* in favor of the term Working Class.

Marxist Usage of Class

In Marxist terms a class is a group of people with a specific relationship to the means of production (social production). Marxists explain history in terms of a war of classes between those who control social production and those who produce social goods. In the Marxist view of capitalism this is a conflict between capitalists (bourgeoisie) and workers (proletariat). Classes are seen as antagonist.

Usage of Class Following Max Weber

When sociologists speak of "class" they usually mean economically based classes in modern or near pre-modern society. Modern usage of the word "class" generally considers only the relative wealth of individuals or social groups, and not the ownership of the means of production.

The sociologist Max Weber formulated a three-component theory of stratification, with class, status and party (or politics) as conceptually distinct elements.

Class is based on relationship to the market (owner, rentier, employee etc.)

Status has to do with honour and prestige

Party refers to factors having to do with affiliations in the political domain.

All three dimensions have consequences for what Weber called "life chances".

Class can be used to describe the stratification of a society. This leads to schemes like the following, relating class to income:

Upper class

Middle class

Lower class

Modern western societies tend to generate a large middle class. Often, class schemes are extend to include sub-classes like "Upper middle class" and "Lower middle class".

Newer sociological theory often sees class as category that isn't very helpful for describing societies. Other approaches include using strata instead of classes, changing the view from objective—income-based—classes to subjective classes, having a look at lifestyle based milieux or discussing different kinds of capital (Bourdieu).

Relevance of Class

At various times the division of society into classes has had various levels of support in law. At one extreme we find old Indian classes - castes, which one could neither enter after birth, nor leave (Though this applied only in relatively recent history.) On the other extreme there exist classes in modern Western societies which appear very fluid and have little support in law. The extent to which classes are important differs also in western societies, e.g. between Great Britain and Scandinavia.

The concept of "caste" differs from that of "class", and refers to rigid status groupings, the membership of which is usually inherited. Particular caste groups include:

the Burakumin of Japan

the *Dalits* ("untouchables") of India

UNTOUCHABLE, DALIT

In India's caste system, an **untouchable**, **dalit**, or **achuta** is a person outside of the four castes, and considered below them. Untouchables include such people as leather-workers. There are various subcastes or jati within untouchable, the lowest ranking generally considered to be the Bhangis.

Harijan was the polite form for *untouchable* coined by Mahatma Gandhi which means "Children of God" (Hari is another name for Vishnu, Hindu God). Untouchables generally consider this term to be condescending and prefer the name **dalit**, variously translated as "*crushed*", "*stepped on*" or "*oppressed*". The term **scheduled castes** is also used in the Indian legal system to refer to this group along with other non-caste tribes.

RACE

This article is about race as a concept of human classification. For the many types of competitive sport, see racing. For an instance of races in the insect world, see List of honeybee races

Race is a type of classification used to group living things based on such elements as common descent, heredity, physical attributes, behavior, economic and academic achievement, and even language. Although the term is sometimes applied to the entire human population ("the human race"), this article is primarily concerned with "race" as the term has been used to designate groups of humans, whether or not the groups are mutually exclusive, and whether or not the classification purports to be objective.

The term *race* is rarely used in contemporary scientific classification, but is sometimes used within, and often outside of, the scientific community in much the same sense as the terms subspecies, population or breed are in biology. It is also common in folk taxonomies and social scientists have argued that it often reflects and is used to legitimize social inequalities. Thus, the use of the word "race" has long been, and remains, controversial. This article reviews debates over the scientific validity of race, the historical construction, social functions, and cultural meanings of racial schemata, and the ethics and politics of the term.

Overview

Many people believe that physical characteristics of various *Homo sapiens* (and, according to some, certain non-physical characteristics such as culture, geography, religion, language and nationality) justify the classification of humanity into various races. This belief emerged during the European Enlightenment and was at that time generally accepted by both the scientific and lay communities.

In the early-to-mid 20th century many biological and social scientists began questioning the accepted causal relationship between biological and cultural attributes, and some began questioning the taxonomic validity of race. In the decades immediately after the Second World War (in which racial theories were used as justification for enormous crimes), and gaining special momentum in the 1960s (in the context of the U.S. civil-rights struggle and global anti-colonial struggle), some came to reject the concept of race as a biological fact altogether, at least as it applies to humans. Nevertheless, the *belief* that human races exist is unquestionably real and, like any belief held by a large number of people, is significant in itself regardless of its scientific accuracy. Thus, the concept continues to impact people through its effect on social behaviour (see communal reinforcement).

In biology, a *race* was defined as a recognisable group forming all or part of a monotypic or polytypic species. A *monotypic* species has no races (this can also be expressed: "*a monotypic species has only one race*"). Monotypic species can occur in several ways:

All members of the species are very similar and cannot be sensibly divided into biologically significant subcategories.

The individuals vary considerably but the variation is essentially random and largely meaningless so far as genetic transmission of these variations is concerned (many plant species fit into this category, which is why horticulturists interested in preserving, say, a particular flower color avoid propagation from seed but instead use vegetative methods like propagation from cuttings).

The variation between individuals is noticeable and does follow a pattern, but there are no clear dividing lines between separate groups: they fade imperceptibly into one another. This is called *clinal variation,* and always indicates substantial gene flow between the apparently separate groups that make up the population(s). Populations that have a steady, substantial gene flow between them are likely to comprise a monotypic species even when a fair degree of surface variation is obvious.

A *polytypic* species, thus, has two or more races (or, in current parlance, two or more "sub-types"). These are separate groups that are clearly distinct from one another and do not generally interbreed (although there may be a relatively narrow hybridization zone), but which *would* interbreed freely if given the chance to do so. Note that groups which would *not* interbreed freely, even if brought together such that they had the opportunity to do so, are not races: they are separate species.

Humans clearly vary considerably. By far the greater part of human genetic variation, however, occurs *within* "racial" groups and the variation *between* racial groups accounts for less than 10% of the total. Nevertheless, although the difference between "races" is less than 10% of the difference within any particular "race", this does not in itself invalidate the suggestion that there might be different races of *Homo sapiens sapiens*. The rules of biological classification do not set any 'smallest allowable difference' between taxa: any distinct difference is sufficient.

However, a distinct difference is only one of the two conditions that must be satisfied before a different form can be classified as a race. The other is lack of significant gene flow between the populations. In the case of human "races", interbreeding is not only possible but widespread.

Given the way that different human "races" fade gradually from one to another in many parts of the world, the overwhelming majority of the current generation of cultural anthropologists draw the conclusion that human "racial" variation is in fact clinal, and that the human species is monotypic. Of course, the delicacy of this definition has left the issue much in debate, especially among physical anthropologists, for if "clines" lead to large areas of separate near-homogeneity, as they seem to do in places like Kenya, Sweden and China, then the people in these areas seem marked off by delimeters resembling nothing so much as the traditional physiological touchstones of "race".

Historians, anthropologists and social scientists today are apt to describe the notion of race as a "social construct", using instead the concept of "population" to refer to communities distinguished by characteristic distributions of gene variants. The concept of biological race, however, has proved resilient and is still used in day-to-day speech even among those who, when questioned, reject the formal existence of race.

This may be a matter of semantics, in that such scientists and laypeople use the word "race" to mean "population", or it may be an effect of the underlying cultural power of the concept of "race" in racist societies. Whether it be "race", "population" or some other appellation, a working concept of sub-specific clustering is crucial because a number of group differences, such as gene mutation profiles strongly linked to certain human subgroups (see Cystic fibrosis, Lactose intolerance, Tay-Sachs Disease and Sickle cell anemia), are difficult to address without recourse to a category higher than "individual" and lower than "species".

HISTORY OF THE TERM

The historical definition of race, before the development of evolutionary biology, was that of common lineage, a vague concept interchangeable with species, breed, cultural origin, or national character ("The whole race of mankind." --Shakespeare; "Whence the long race of Alban fathers come" --Dryden).

The word *race* in this general sense of a group of people with common descent was introduced into English in about 1580.

This late origin is consistent with the thesis that the concept of "race" as defining a very small number of groups based on greatly separated lines of descent dates at least in the West from the time of Columbus. Older concepts that were also at least partly based on common descent, such as nation and tribe, entail a much larger number of groupings.

In any case, the first published classification of humans into distinct "races" seems to have been François Bernier's *Nouvelle division de la terre par les différents espèces ou races qui l'habitent* ("New division of Earth by the different species or races which inhabit it"), which appeared in a Parisian journal in 1684. Bernier (1625-1688) distinguished four "races":

Europeans, including South Asians, North Africans and native Americans, but excluding Lapps

Far Easterners

Sub-Saharan Africans

Lapps

The 19th-century concept of *race* was based primarily on morphological and cosmetic characteristics such as skin color, facial type, cranial profile and amount, texture and color of hair. Though such characteristics have since been declared by many experts to have a minimal relationship with any other heritable characteristics, they retain some persuasive force because it is easy to immediately distinguish people based on physical appearance.

Because people of different races can interbreed, this method of classification is weak (compare with species). In other words, *racial purity* does not have a clear biological meaning. On the other hand, it is clear that for an extended period of time after *Homo sapiens*' first migrations from Africa (probably around 80,000 BC) and before the rise of wheeled and seagoing transportation (around 3000 BC), geographically isolated groups of people underwent some degree of divergent evolution.

Whether that degree was high enough to merit strict taxa beneath the species level is the primary question that has roiled the generations of human biologists since the 1800s. It is a complicated issue full of semantic and emotional pitfalls, with much at stake on the consensus, for educators, physicians, political officeholders, judges, law enforcement officers and many others look upon scientific findings as the bedrock authority for their curricula, diagnostic methods, budget expenditures, case law and criminal suspect profiling.

Among the 19th-century naturalists who defined the field were Georges Cuvier, James Cowles Pritchard, Louis Agassiz, Charles Pickering (*Races of Man and Their Geographical Distribution*, 1848), and Johann Friedrich Blumenbach. Cuvier enumerated three races, Pritchard seven, Agassiz eight, and Pickering eleven. Blumenbach's classification was widely adopted:

1. the Caucasian, or white race, to which belong the greater part of the European nations and those of Western Asia
2. the Mongolian, or yellow race, occupying Tartary, China, Japan, etc.
3. the Ethiopian, or black race, occupying most of Africa (except the north), Australia, New Guinea and other Pacific Islands

4. the American, or red race, comprising the Indians of North and South America
5. the Malayan, or brown race, which occupies the islands of the Indian Archipelago

Researchers in the decades following Blumenbach classified the Malay and American races as branches of the Mongolian, leaving only the Caucasian, Mongolian, and Ethiopian races. Further explication in the early and mid twentieth century, notably by American anthropologist Carleton S. Coon, arrived at three primary races (Negroid, Caucasoid, Sinoid) with a small number of less widespread races (especially "Australoid").

In Blumenbach's day, physical characteristics like skin color, cranial profile, etc., went hand in hand with declarations of group character and aptitude. The "fairness" and relatively high brows of "caucasians" were held to be apt physical expressions of a loftier mentality and a more generous spirit.

The epicanthic folds around the eyes of "mongolians" and their slightly sallow outer epidermal layer bespoke their supposedly crafty, literal-minded nature. The dark skin and relatively sloping craniums of "ethiopians" were taken as wholesale proof of a closer genetic proximity to the primates, despite the fact that the skin of chimpanzees and gorillas beneath the hair is whiter than the average "caucasian" skin and that orangutans and some monkey species have foreheads fully as vertical as the typical Englishman or German. By Coon's day, group physical characteristics were, for the most part, unhitched from assessments of group character and aptitude. Since Coon, those who merely maintain the reality of moderately distinct group physical traits are closely watched as likely carriers of the old malign racism.

Modern criticism of the biological significance of "race" can be dated to the publication in 1935 of a book by Julian Huxley and A.C. Haddon: *We Europeans: a survey of "racial" problems* (London: Jonathan Cape, 1935).

Politics of Race

The concept of race was applied at the time of Blumenbach by political theorists such as Johann Gottfried von Herder to nationalist theory to develop a militant ethnic nationalism. They posited the historical existence of "races" such as the German and French race, branching from basal races supposed to have existed for millennia, such as the "Aryan" race, and believed political boundaries should mirror these racial boundaries. Later, one of Hitler's favorite sayings was "Politics is applied biology".

Hitler's pseudoscientific ideas of racial purity led to atrocities on an unprecedented scale, and "racial cleansing" or "ethnic cleansing" as a sociopolitical motivation or justification has reared its head several times since Hitler (particularly in Cambodia, the Balkans and East Africa). In one sense, such "cleansing" is merely another name for the tribal warfare and mass murder that has afflicted human society from time out of mind. But these crimes seem to gain an extra intensity and thoroughness when the perpetrators believe their acts are sanctioned on scientific grounds.

Racial inequality has been a concern of United States politicians and legislators since the country's founding. In the 19th century most "white" Americans (including abolitionists) explained racial inequality as an inevitable consequence of biological differences. In the second half of the 20th century, political and civic leaders as well as scientists debated whether racial inequality is biological or cultural in origin.

On one end of the political spectrum, some argued that current inequalities between blacks and whites are primarily cultural and historical, the result of such historical wrongs as slavery and segregation, and could be redressed through such programs as "affirmative action" and "Head Start." On the other end of the spectrum, a movement to redirect tax money away from remedial programs for minority phenotypes was based on interpretations of aptitude test data which, according to advocates, showed that race-linked differences in basic ability are biological in origin and cannot be leveled even by intensive educational efforts. In electoral politics, many more members of racial and ethnic minorities have won important offices in western nations compared to earlier times, although the very highest offices tend to remain in the hands of racial/ethnic majorities.

Religious leaders active in the United States began to decry segregation and discrimination based on race in the latter half of the 20th century. The Rev. Dr. Martin Luther King famously requested people to form a society where people were judged "on the content of their character, not the color of their skin." The Rev. Sun Myung Moon said, "With respect to races, inferiority or superiority doesn't exist. Color counts for nothing."

Anthropological and Genetic Studies of Race

In the 19th century many natural scientists made three claims about race: first, that races are objective, naturally occurring things; second, that there is a strong relationship between biological races and other human phenomena (such as social behavior and culture, and by extension the relative material success of cultures); third, that race is therefore a valid scientific category that can be used to explain and predict individual and group behavior. In the 20th century, mainstream anthropologists and others rejected each of these claims, while continuing to study between-group genotypic and phenotypic variations.

By the end of the 20th century, most social and many natural scientists turned to the "population" concept to talk about these variations, arguing that accounts of "race" (within both the popular and scientific literatures) are socially constructed. Some social and natural scientists, however, argue that new studies in molecular genetics support a nomenclature strongly reminiscent of traditional racial and ethnic terminology.

Since human beings are the most complex entities we know of, the empirical study of man is in many ways the most difficult of all, making problems in fields like physics and chemistry look elementary in comparison. It is no surprise that fields like anthropology, human genetics and psychology are in flux, and the state of these fields may change radically during this century as advances in the more elementary sciences are synthesized into increasingly objective definitions of "human nature". Recognition of sub-specific group traits may find a place in these definitions, probably without, however, the valuations of overall superiority and inferiority formerly attached to them.

A rejection of 19th century assumptions was initiated by Franz Boas, the founder of American academic anthropology.[1] In the first decades of the 20th century he studied the relationship between race and height in New York City, discovering that the children of immigrants were taller than their parents. Although height is clearly primarily a biological phenomenon, he concluded that an individual's height was determined not only by inheritance but by environment as well (in this case, better pre- and neo-natal care, especially nutrition). Since height, even after accounting for environmental factors, is still at least 80%

heritable, and since human subgroup height averages irreducibly differ according to that hard genetic determinant, many of Boas's students accepted the existence of race as a biological fact. But they concluded that there was no relationship between biological race and other human phenomena (such as social behavior, culture, intelligence and morality).

By the 1950s anthropologists had come to question the very existence of race as a biological phenomenon. This rejection was based on three facts. First, they pointed out that the preponderance of evidence suggests that all human beings are descended from a common ancestor (although this fact alone has little bearing on the subsequent formation or non-formation of new subgroups). Second, they observed that there are many biological differences between people that are not taken into account by race (for example, blood type).

Finally, they pointed out that oftentimes the genetic differences between members of the same race are greater than the average genetic difference between races. For example, the variation in blood types within specific groups is 85%, but the total variation between groups is only 15% (see the American Anthropological Association's Statement on Race. Those who continue to believe in the real existence of biological race, or in genetic clusters similar to race, point out that in determining overall relatedness the entire genetic cohorts of groups must be compared. When this is done, a grouping pattern emerges that closely follows traditional race groupings.

For example, it is true that the so-called "Negroid" race contains more in-group variation than the other major races. Great differences in height, for instance, can be found within a small geographical area (the "pygmies" are the shortest people in the world on average, while their neighbors, formerly known as "the Watusi", are the tallest). These two "negroid" subgroups vary more from each other in height than either does with the averages for height in the other two major races. However, if total genetic cohorts are used rather than limited sets of traits like height and blood type in an effort to find true overall relatedness, it is seen that any two "negroids" will share a much higher net genetic affinity with one another than either will with any individual of the other two major races. The same is true for any two caucasoids and any two sinoids (see conclusions of the Human Population Genetics Laboratory headed by L. Luca Cavalli-Sforza at).

These developments had important consequences. For example, some scientists developed the notion of "population" to take the place of race. This substitution is not simply a matter of exchanging one word for another. Populations are, in a sense, simply statistical clusters that emerge from the choice of variables of interest; there is no preferred set of variables.

The "populationist" view does not deny that there are physical differences among people; it simply claims that the historical conceptions of "race" are not particularly useful in analyzing these differences scientifically. In particular, populationists claim that:

1. knowing someone's "race" does not provide very good predictive information about biological characteristics other than those that have been selected to define the racial categories, e.g. knowing a person's skin color, which is generally acknowledged to be one of the markers of race (or taken as a defining characteristic of race), does not allow good predictions of a person's blood type to be made;

2. in general, the natural distribution of human phenotypes exhibits gradual trends of difference across geographic zones, not the categorical differences of race; in particular, there are many peoples (like the San of S. W. Africa, or the people of northern India) who have phenotypes that do not neatly fit into the standard race categories.
3. focusing on race has historically led not only to seemingly insoluble disputes about classification (e.g. are the Japanese a distinct race, a mixture of races, or part of the East Asian race? and what about the Ainu?) but has also exposed disagreement about the criteria for making decisions— the selection of phenotypic traits seemed arbitrary.

Since the 1960s, some anthropologists and teachers of anthropology have re-conceived "race" as a cultural category or social construct, in other words, as a particular way some people have of talking about themselves and others. As such it cannot be a useful analytical concept; rather, the use of the term "race" itself must be analyzed. Moreover, biology will not explain why or how people use the idea of race: history and social relationships will.

A smaller number of anthropologists and human geneticists argue that race is indeed a valid and valuable concept and that those holding the majority view allow their social consciences (laudable per se) to confuse and delay accurate interpretations and applications of empirical data. They are not convinced by the substitution of the term "population" for the term "race", because it leads to a potentially harmful imprecision in communication (for example, when one could simply say "caucasian" one is instead compelled to say something like "an individual of the western Eurasian population", and when that individual doesn't happen to currently reside in western Eurasia one must say "an individual whose ancestors were of the western Eurasian population").

This position recently received a boost from genetic studies at the molecular level which show characteristic allele signatures for the groups traditionally identified as the three major races, resulting in maps that clearly delineate *genetic clines* (in which the clinal zones are a small part of the total) summarized quite well by longstanding racial and ethnic appellations. Precision and commonality in terminological communication is especially important in fields like medical research and diagnosis because a rapidly growing list of genetic disorders and predispositions are strongly linked to race and ethnicity (not to geographical "populations").

If "races" is too freighted a term for these clines then, according to these authorities, new, convenient, non-academic terminology free of spurious valuations of superiority and inferiority should be developed whether social sensitivities are ruffled or not.

Two examples, one from the United States and one from Brazil, further illustrate the majority view.

Example : United States

In the **United States** in the 19th century, African-Americans, Native Americans, and European-Americans were each classified as different races. But the criteria for membership in these races were radically different. The government considered anyone with "one drop" of Black blood to be Black. In contrast, Indians were defined by a certain percentage of "Indian blood". And to be White one had to have "pure" White ancestry. These differing criteria for membership in particular races has little to do with biology and much to do with political relations between Blacks and Indians on the one hand, and Whites on the other. By these criteria, it was very easy for a child to be categorized as Black. This likely reflects the requirements of the slave-economy of the U.S. South, for the vast majority of slaves were classified as Black. Even the child of an enslaved African woman and a White master was considered Black, or "of African descent." More importantly, such a child would be a slave.

In comparison, it was harder for a child to be classified as Indian. After a few generations of inter-racial marriages, a child might not be considered Indian at all. This likely reflects the requirements of the U.S. economy during the period of westward expansion, although the greater outward similarity of "Whites" and "Indians" surely came into it. Indians had treaty rights to land, but if an individual with one Indian great-grandparent was no longer classified as Indian, they would lose special rights to land. At a time when Whites ruled both Blacks and Indians, it is no coincidence that the hardest race to prove membership in was White.

Example: Brazil

Compared to 19th century United States, 20th century **Brazil** was characterized by a relative absence of sharply defined racial groups. This pattern reflects a different history and different social relations. Basically, race in Brazil was biologized, but in a way that recognized the difference between ancestry (which determines genotype) and phenotypic differences. There, racial identity was not governed by a rigid descent rule. A Brazilian child was never automatically identified with the racial type of one or both parents, nor were there only two categories to chose from. Over a dozen racial categories would be recognized in conformity with the combinations of hair color, hair texture, eye color, and skin color. These types grade into each other like the colors of the spectrum and no one category stands significantly isolated from the rest. That is, race referred to appearance, not heredity.

One of the most striking consequences of the Brazilian system of racial identification was that parents and children and even brothers and sisters were frequently accepted as representatives of opposite racial types. In a fishing village in the state of Bahia an investigator showed 100 people pictures of three sisters and were asked to identify the races of each. In only six responses were the sisters identified by the same racial term.

Fourteen responses used a different term for each sister. In another experiment nine portraits were shown to a hundred people. Forty different racial types were elicited. It was found, in addition, that a given Brazilian might be called by as many as thirteen different terms by other members of the community. These terms are spread out across practically the entire spectrum of theoretical racial types. A further consequence of the absence of a descent rule was that Brazilians apparently not only disagreed about the racial identity of specific individuals, but they also seemed to be in disagreement about the abstract meaning of the racial terms as defined by words and phrases. For example, 40% of a sample ranked moreno claro as a lighter type than mulato claro, while 60% reversed this order.

A further note of confusion is that one person might employ different racial terms for another person over a short time. The use of term varies with the personal relationship and mood. Consequently, people change their racial identity over their lifetimes. This is not the same as "passing" in the USA. It does not require secrecy and the agonizing withdrawal from friends and family that are necessary in this country and among Indians of highland Latin America. In Brazil passing from one race to another occurs with changes in education and economic status. A light skinned person of low status is considered darker than a dark skinned person of high status.

So although the identification of a person by race is far more fluid and flexible in Brazil than in the USA, there are racial stereotypes and prejudices. African features were considered less desirable; Blacks were considered inferior, and Whites superior. These stereotypes are obvious relics of the slave-based plantation system, and say more about history than actual behavior. But the complexity of racial classification in Brazil bears testimony not only to the amount of intermarriage in the post-slavery period, but also to the possibilities of upward mobility.

A Brazilian is never merely black or white or some other race; he is rich, well-educated, or poor and uneducated. It makes more sense to say that it is one's class and not one's appearance that determines who will be admitted to hotels, restaurants, and social clubs; who will get preferential treatment in stores, churches, and hotels; and who will have the best chance among a group of marriage suitors – and color is one of the criteria of class identity, but it is not the only one. (This case is taken from Marvin Harris' excellent short study, *Patterns of Race in the Americas*)

Race and Intelligence

Many researchers have proposed and studied possible relationships between race and intelligence. While such proposals have a long history, some contemporary experts argue that they have always been wrong; see the *American*

Anthropological Association's Statement on Race and Intelligence. A well-known, strong dissent to this opinion can be found in the works of Arthur Jensen, Professor of Educational Psychology at the University of California, Berkeley. Jensen's extensive primary research in the field has, he claims, found a high heritability of "the intelligence factor" with statistically significant genotype-based variation between populations.

In his book *The Mismeasure of Man*, Stephen Jay Gould, a Harvard paleontologist better known for his popularizing articles in *Natural History* Magazine (which have been collected in a variety of mass-marketed books) makes three criticisms of Jensen's work. The first criticism is also the criticism most commonly leveled against Jensen by other anthropologists and biologists: that Jensen misunderstands the concept of "heritability." Heritability measures the percentage of variation of a trait due to inheritance, *within* a population. Jensen, however, has used the concept of heritability to measure differences in inheritance *between* populations (Gould 1981: 127; 156-156).

The second criticism is relatively minor: Gould disagrees with Jensen's support of the attempts of others to calculate the IQ of dead people (such as the famous Polish astronomer and Prussian monetary theorist Copernicus) (1981: 153-154). The third criticism is significant: Gould disagrees with Jensen's belief that IQ tests measure a real variable called *g* or "general intelligence," which can be measured along a unilinear scale. This is a claim most closely identified with Cyril Burt and Charles Spearman. According to Gould, Jensen misunderstood the research of L. L. Thurstone to ultimately support this claim; Gould however argues that Thurstone's factoral analysis of intelligence revealed *g* to be an illusion (1981: 159; 13-314).

Jensen made a strong reply to Gould in the summer 1982 issue of *Contemporary Education Review* (see [3]), where he states "Gould claims that I have defended a g, or general intelligence, which is 'reified as a measurable object'. Yet in the same chapter from which Gould is supposedly paraphrasing my views (Jensen, 1980a), I stated unequivocally that 'Intelligence is not an entity, but a theoretical construct.... The g factor may also be termed a theoretical construct, which is intended to explain an observable phenomenon, namely, the positive intercorrelation among all mental tests, regardless of their apparently great variety'".

Phylogenetic Representations

Recent genetic analyses have enabled the concept of race to be represented in somewhat cladistic terms. These studies have indicated that, as already known, Africa was the ancestral source of all people. Australian aborigines were found to be an early out-group that remained isolated. All other groups, including Caucasians, Asians, and Native Americans, were found to be a single related (monophyletic) group resulting from a later out-migration from Africa, which could reasonably be divided into more or less the equivalents of Caucasian and Sinoid groups, although, of course, recognizing that there are many intermediates.

Here the problem arises of distinguishing black Africans as a racial group; it doesn't work because it is a paraphyletic classification—that is, to take black Africans as a racial group, the group by definition includes every living person on Earth because everyone is descended from this group. And, of course, it has long been known that groups such as the Khoi-San are as different from other sub-Saharan groups as are Caucasians and Asians.

Related Concepts

ethnicity, multiracial, master race, racism, race card, race relations, racial equality, racial purity, racial discrimination, racial superiority.

Because individual geography, culture, religion, political association and, above all, heredity can change, *racial purity*, the concept that wholly distinct racial groupings exist, has little meaning from the perspective of evolutionary biology.

Indeed, it is possibly preferable in many situations (if not all) to think in terms of ethnicity (a term without the implication of continental groupings, but rather of smaller geographic area with more homogeneity and clearer definition) than of race; there is less question as to the validity of ethnicity.

Ergo, you have Britons, Frenchmen, Germans, Poles, et al. rather than thinking of "Caucasians," a term implying a possible ancestor group in the Caucasus that is too distant for much consideration and moreover reaching to groups including Jews, Arabs, Persians, and others that differ notably, both culturally and to a lesser yet still noteworthy extent physically, from the aforementioned ethnic groups There can be as much difference between two ethnicities grouped into a "race" as between either of those and an ethnic group grouped (often arbitrarily) into another "race."

Note: This article is in the process of revision. The proposed new text is followed by the original article, portions of which will later be moved to other articles.

A person's **gender role** is made up of all of the things a person does to express their gender identity. It then becomes the set of signals by which others infer that persons gender identity. For instance, if someone identifies themselves as a girl or woman, then they will ordinarily do the kind of things that will let other people know that they are a girl or woman. And, if someone identifies themselves as a boy or man then they will ordinarily do the kind of things that will let other people know that they are a boy or man. A man who wants to attract girlfriends would rarely if ever use his clothing, behavior, etc., to present himself in the guise of a woman. Similarly, a woman would ordinary be ill-advised to seek a man by presenting herself in the guise of a man.

In most cases, when a man appears in the guise of a woman, or a woman appears in the guise of a man, then most people will agree that they are disguising themselves, that is, that they are engaged in deliberately deceptive behavior. (Because many societies impose expectations on the behavior of the members of society, and the expectations are linked to the gender identities of those individuals, there are prescriptions regarding gender roles, i.e., expectations that men and women will hold different kinds of positions in society.

Failure to comply with these expectations can produce a wide range of sanctions.) It should be noted that some societies are comparatively rigid in their expectations, and other societies are comparatively permissive. Some of the gender signals that form part of a gender role and indicate one's gender identity to others are quite obvious, and others are so subtle that they are transmitted and received out of ordinary conscious awareness.

Some elements of gender role are connected with body differences related to sex. For instance, women's blouses make room for women's breasts and do not have pockets that cover the nipples. Men's shirts, essentially the same garment, are flatter and do have pockets over the nipples.

Men frequently find it convenient to urinate while standing, but women rarely do. Women frequently nurse infants. Men have mammary glands but they only very rarely nurse infants because the special hormonal states that produce lactation usually follow only from pregnancy.See male_lactation.

Another set of gender roles are related to body differences related to sex, but the body differences are things like height and muscular strength for which there is a substantial overlap of the abilities of men and women. Some women are stronger than some men. Some women are larger and/or taller than some men. But if you average the heights of all men and the heights of all women, they won't be equal. If you are looking for the world champion weight lifter, it is unlikely that it will be a woman.

In many societies, there is a strong tendency to exaggerate gender role differences. Starting with the belief that men are generally stronger than women, people conclude, somehow, that men should be stronger than women, and that there is something inadequate about a man who is not very strong. Starting with the belief that women are generally more gentle and nurturing than men, people construct a socially supported ideal that says that women should be gentle and nurturing and should not be harsh or aggressive. Many societies jump from the observation that men are less likely to cry than are women to the practice of indoctrinating boys, virtually from birth, not to cry.

Some gender role differences are purely conventional. That is, they work the way laws about which side of the street to drive on work. As long as everyone in Great Britain drives on the left side of the road, and as long as everyone in the United States drives on the right side of the road, there will be no problem with head-on collisions. In most societies, men wear trousers and women wear skirts. But in a traditional Malay community it is an ordinary practice for men to wear sarongs. In the traditional society of Scotland, men wore kilts. As long as the cultural context matches the choice of clothing it would be unusual for any negative comment to arise in such cases.

Gender role differences that are purely conventional are easier to change than are those that have some link to the biology of individuals. One consequence of social unrest during the Vietnam War era in the United States, Great Britain, and many other countries, was that men began to let their hair grow to a length that was previously considered appropriate only to women. Somewhat later, in response to other social changes, many women began to cut their hair to lengths previously considered appropriate only to men. The practical consequences of these changes were not onerous.

It would, to the contrary, be rather more difficult to get men to give up trousers that have a zipper that facilitates urinating while standing. It would likewise be difficult to get women to wear tight-fitting fly fishermen's vests made of nylon netting with a half-inch mesh. Such a garment, regardless of how stylish it might be considered one fine year, would be too uncomfortable for a woman to wear unless she first bound her breasts with some other fabric to protect them from rubbing against the harsh netting and pocket contents of the vest.

Biological factors sometimes have a strong impact on which occupations are judged by a society to be appropriate for men, and which are judged appropriate for women. There is no reason why a large woman could not successfully shoe horses or deliver freight shipments from railway stations to the recipients' homes. However, there are not even very many men who have the strength and stamina to put shoes on an uncooperative Clydesdale draft horse. Societies seem to frequently jump from a valid observation to a false conclusion in cases such as these. A society may jump from the observation that only a very few women would be physically suited to shoe a heavy draft horse to the conclusion that no woman should be a farrier, of jump from the observation that only a few women would be physically suited to serve as a fireman to the conclusion that women should not be eligible to apply for those jobs.

In many other cases, the elements of convention or tradition seem to play a dominant role in deciding which occupations fit in with which gender roles. In the United States, physicians have traditionally been men, and the few people who defied that expectation received a special job description: "woman doctor." Similarly, we have special terms like "male nurse," "woman lawyer," "lady barber," etc. But in China and the former Soviet Union countries, medical doctors are predominantly women, and in Taiwan it is very common for all of the barbers in a barber shop to be women.

As long as a person's external genitals are consistent with that person's gender identity the gender role of a person is so much a matter of course in a stable society that people rarely even think of it unless for whatever reason an individual adopts a gender role that is inconsistent with his or her gender identity. When that kind of thing happens, it is most often done to deliberately provoke a sense of incongruity and a humorous reaction to the attempts of a person of one sex trying to pass himself or herself off as a member of another sex. People can find much entertainment in observing the exaggerations or the failures to get nuances of an unfamiliar gender role right.

It is not so entertaining, however, when the external genitalia of a person, that person's gender identity, and/or that person's gender role are not consistent. People naturally, but too easily, assume that if a person has a penis, scrotum, etc., then that person is chromosomally male (i.e., that person has one X chromosome and one Y chromosome), and that the person, in introspection, feels like a male. Mother nature is much more inventive than is our language and system of traditional concepts. The person may have a penis and scrotum, but may be a female (with XX chromosomal sexual identity) with normal female sexual organs internally. When that person reaches puberty, "his" breasts may enlarge to ordinary female proportions, and "he" may begin to menstruate, passing menstrual blood through "his" penis. In addition, this person may have always accepted a gender identity that is consistent with "his" external genitalia or with "her" internal genitalia.

Just as there are individuals whose external genitalia make them falsely appear to be male, there are also individuals whose external genitalia make them falsely appear to be females. There are individuals whose genitalia are intermediate in appearance between those of an ordinary male and those of an ordinary female. An examination of their chromosomal sex and/or other tests may be necessary to determine what these people really are. And there are even individuals who have both male and female sexual organs in the same body.

When we consider these more unusual products of Mother Nature's inventiveness, the simple picture that we saw in which there was a high degree of consistency among external genitalia, gender identity, and gender role then dissolves into a kind of jigsaw puzzle that is difficult to put together correctly. The extra parts of this jigsaw puzzle fall into two closely related categories, atypical gender identities and atypical gender roles.

Such incidents are rare. For the vast majority of people their gender *is* commensurate with their genitalia.

Language is a system of abstractions and frequently deals with idealized cases. The more sharply masculine gender roles are distinguished from feminine gender roles, the less likely it is that any individual human being will comply perfectly with the requirements of that gender role. And besides that fact, every individual in a society is likely to have his or her unique definition of the "proper masculine gender role" and the "proper feminine gender role."

Any individual, then, might well be expected to be in compliance with the gender role ideals held by some people and to fail to be in compliance with the gender role ideals held by some other people. When, for instance, a boy cries too readily for the tastes of some people, they will call the child a "sissy" to indicate that in their view he is not a very ideal boy. There are many such pejorative role-related terms.

GENDER ROLES

Sociologists and sexologists use the term **gender roles** to name the behaviors and responsibilities prescribed for each gender by a society.

Cultural Views of Gender Roles

Ideas of appropriate behavior according to gender vary between cultures, although some aspects receive more widespread attention than others. For example, in most current and known historical cultures, martial combat has been seen as mostly (or only) appropriate for men, while child-rearing has been seen as mostly (or only) the domain of women.

Other aspects, however, may differ markedly with time and place. In pre-industrial Europe, for example, the practice of medicine (other than midwifery) was generally seen as a male prerogative. However, in Russia health care was more often seen as a feminine role. The results of these views can be seen in modern society, where European medicine is most often practiced by men, while the majority of Russian doctors are women.

Another Nature Versus Nurture Debate

Considerable debate exists as to whether gender roles are biologically mandated, in the sense of the behavioral traits arising primarily from the biology of sex; or culturally mandated, in the sense of behavioral traits arising from early socialization. As with many such debates, most researchers believe that both factors influence the development and propagation of gender roles. However, the relative influence of each, and the specifics of how that influence operates, are still hotly disputed.

Examples of Western Gender Roles

In the early 20th century, western gender roles were based around the idea of heteronormativity, and as such they were comparatively fixed. People who transgressed gender roles, such as a women with high-powered jobs, frequently experienced disapproval and discrimination.

Some examples of commonly seen gender role descriptions:

- A man, is someone who enjoys sex, has a career, and has difficulty expressing his emotions.
- A woman, is someone who wears cosmetics, and wants to get married, start a family and be a housewife.

- An effeminate man, is a man who is more or less like a stereotypical woman.
- A girl, is someone who wears skirts and dresses, plays with dolls, likes the colour pink, has long hair, and wants to wear make-up.
- A tomboy, is a girl who behaves like a stereotypical boy.
- A boy, is someone who wears rugged clothing, likes the colour blue, plays with toy soldiers, participates in competitive team sports, enjoys fighting, doesn't cry, and has short hair.
- A sissy, is a boy who behaves like a stereotypical girl.

After the sexual revolution, gay liberation, and feminism movements of the mid to late 20th century (the 1960s in particular), new roles became available in Western societies, and gender roles became rather more flexible. Narrowly defined gender roles, such as those listed here, are generally recognised as stereotypes.

Other Stereotypes

Man

Head and breadwinner of the family

Responsible for contacts outward

Strong, rational, sexually active

Men as "hunters"

Woman

Dependent on and subject to a male commander (father, husband etc..)

Responsible for the social connections within the family

Weak, emotional and irrational, compensatorily, sexually passive or uninterested.

CULTURE

There are separate pages about "The Culture" in the novels of Iain M. Banks and about the sociological term "Cultural Creatives". Another one is about the Jamaican reggae group; see Culture (band).

The word **culture** comes from the Latin root *colere,* to inhabit, cultivate, or honor. In general it refers to human activity; different definitions of *culture* reflect different theories for understanding, or criteria for valuing, human activity. In 1952 Alfred Kroeber and Clyde Kluckhohn compiled a list of over 200 different definitions of *culture* in their book, *Culture: A Critical Review of Concepts and Definitions.*

The popular use of the word *culture* in many Western societies reflects the fact that these societies are stratified. Many use the word *culture* to refer to elite consumption goods and activities such as fine cuisine, art, and music. Some label this as **"high" culture** to distinguish it from **"low" culture**, meaning non-elite consumption goods and activities.

18th and early 19th century scholars, and many people today, often identified culture with "civilization" and opposed both to "nature." Thus, people lacking elements of "high culture" were often considered to be more "natural," and elements of high culture were often criticized, or defended, for repressing human nature.

By the late nineteenth century, anthropologists argued for a broader definition of *culture* that they could apply to a wide variety of societies, they began to argue that culture *is* human nature, and is rooted in the universal human capacity to classify experiences, and encode and communicate them symbolically. Consequently, people living apart from one another develop unique cultures, but elements of different cultures can easily spread from one group of people to another.

Anthropologists have thus had to develop methodologically and theoretically useful definitions of the word. Technically, anthropologists distinguish between **material culture** and **symbolic culture**, not only because each reflects different kinds of human activity but because they consitutc different kinds of data that require different methodologies. As a rule, archeologists focus on material culture, and cultural anthropologists focus on symbolic culture, although ultimately both groups are interested in the relationship between these two dimensions.

Moreover, anthropologists understand "culture" to refer not only to consumption goods, but to the general processes by which such goods are produced and given meaning, and the social relationships and practices in which such objects and processes are embedded.

In the early twentieth century anthropologists understood culture to refer not to a set of discrete products or activities (whether material or symbolic) but rather to underlying patterns of products and activities. Moreover, they assumed that such patterns were clearly bounded (thus, some people confuse "culture" for the society that has a particular culture). In smaller societies in which people were divided by age, gender, household, and descent group, anthropologists believed that people more or less shared the same set of values and conventions. In larger societies in which people were further divided by region, race or ethnicity, and class, they believed that members of the same society often had highly contrasting values and conventions. They thus used the term **subculture** to identify the cultures of parts of larger societies. Since subcultures reflect the position of a segment of society vis a vis other segments and the society as a whole, they often reveal processes of domination and resistance.

Cultural studies developed in the late 20th century, in part through the reintroduction of Marxist thought in sociology, and in part through the articulation of sociology and other academic disciplines such as literary criticism, in order to focus on the analysis of subcultures in capitalist societies. Following the non-anthropological tradition, cultural studies generally focus on the study of consumption goods (such as fashion, art, and literature). Because the 18th and 19th century distinction between "high" and "low" culture is not appropriate to the mass-produced and mass-marketed consumption goods with which cultural studies is concerned, these scholars refer instead to **popular culture**.

Today some anthropologists have joined the project of cultural studies. Most, however, reject the identification of culture with consumption goods. Furthermore, many now reject the notion of culture as bounded, and consequently reject the notion of subculture. Instead, they see culture as a complex web of shifting patterns that link people in different locales, and link social formations of different scales.

CULTURE THEORY

Culture theory is that branch of anthropology and other related social science disciplines (i.e., for example, sociology) that seeks to define the heuristic concept of culture in operational and/or scientific terms. In the 19th century culture was used by some to refer to a wide array of human activities, and by others as a synonym for "civilization". In the 20th century, anthropologists began theorizing about culture as an object of scientific analysis. Some used it to distinguish human adaptive strategies from the largely instinctive adaptive strategies of animals, including the adaptive strategies of other primates and non-human hominids, whereas others used it to refer to symbolic representations and expressions of human experience, with no direct adaptive value. Both groups understood culture as being definitive of human nature.

According to many theories that have gained wide acceptance among anthropologists, culture exhibits the way that humans interpret their biology and their environment. According to this point of view, culture becomes such an integral part of human existence that it *is* the human environment, and most cultural change can be attributed to human adaptation to historical events.

Moreover, given that culture is seen as the primary adaptive mechanism of humans and takes place much faster than human biological evolution, most cultural change can be viewed as culture adapting to itself.

Although most anthropologists try to define culture in such a way that it separates human beings from other animals, many human traits are similar to those of other animals, particularly the traits of other primates. For example, chimpanzees have big brains, but *ceteris paribus* human brains are bigger. Similarly, bonobos exhibit complex sexual behavior, but human beings exhibit much more complex sexual behaviors.

As such, anthropologists often debate whether human behavior is different from animal behavior in degree rather than in kind; they must also find ways to distinguish cultural behavior from sociological behavior and psychological behavior.

Cultural Behavior

Cultural behavior is behavior exhibited by human beings (and, some would argue, by other species as well, though to a much lesser degree) that is extrasomatic or extragenetic, in other words, learned

Learned Behaviour

There is a species of ant that builds nests made of leaves. To build a nest, some of these ants pull the edges of two leaves together and hold them in place, while others carry larva in their jaws and 'sew' them together with the silk they secrete. This is certainly a complex feat of engineering, but it is not cultural. This behaviour is instinctive, built into the ants' behaviour mechanisms. The cannot alter their plans or think of better ways to join leaves. They cannot teach or be taught to do so.

But there are examples of animals that can learn behaviours, such as dogs. A dog doesn't know instinctively not to urinate or defecate indoors, but it can be taught not to do so. Dogs are capable of learning specific behaviours.

Concepts, Generalisations, Abstractions and Ideas

A dog's acquisition of a behaviour satisfies one of the requirements of culture, but it also fulfills another. If you were to take a dog that has learned not to eliminate indoors to a different house, it would still know not to eliminate there. This is because the dog has made a generalization. It knows not to urinate or defecate in any house, not just the one in which it was taught. However, this behaviour only makes two of the four requirements.

Behaviour Shared through Extragenetic Transmission

For a behaviour to be considered cultural it must be shared extragenetically; that is, it must be taught. If a trained dog is introduced to a puppy that doesn't know not to eliminate in a house, it cannot teach it not to do so. A particularly intelligent puppy might eventually learn not to eliminate in people's houses by observing the older dog, but no active teaching would have taken place.

Contrast this with an observed group of Macaque monkeys. Some scientists wanted to learn about eating behaviours in Macaque monkeys, so they put some sweet potatoes on a beach near where they lived. The sweet potatoes got sandy and, as the monkeys disliked dirty food, they would spend some time picking the sand off. One young female, however started taking her potatoes to a freshwater pool to rinse off. She showed the others how to do so as well. The scientists then threw wheat on the sand, hoping the monkeys would spend more time picking the food out so they would have more time to observe them. The same young female just scooped up handfuls of wheat and sand and dumped them in the water. The sand sank and the wheat floated, which she ate. This practice also quickly spread through the group. This is what we could call a proto-cultural behaviour. It is learned, it involves concepts and generalisations, and it is taught. There is only one thing missing.

Artifacts, Concrete and Abstract

Cultural behaviour must involve the use of artifacts. The most famous example in the animal world is the termite stick. Some chimpanzees in Tanzania have learned to fish termites out of their nests using sticks. They select a stick and modify it to fit down an opening in a termite nest, insert it, wiggle it around and withdraw it, eating the termites that have attacked the stick and stuck to it. This fits our criteria for cultural behaviour. It is not genetically programmed. Not all chimps do it, as would happen if it were built into the chimps' genes. It involves several complex generalisations and ideas, involving understanding the termites' behaviour and how to exploit it, and conceiving of a tool with which to do so. It is taught by mother chimps to their offspring. And it involves the use of an artifact: the stick itself.

The difference between the culture of our species and the behaviours exhibited by others is that humans cannot survive without culture. Everything we see, touch, interact with and think about is cultural. It is the major adaptive mechanism for our species. We cannot survive winters in upper latitudes without protective clothing and shelter, which are provided culturally. We cannot obtain food without being taught how. Whereas other organisms that exhibit cultural behaviour don't necessarily need it for the perpetuation of their species, we absolutely cannot live without it.

Language is an important element in human culture. It is the primary abstract artifact by which culture is transmitted extragenetically (fulfilling points 3 and 4). Only so much can be shown, much more must be explained. Most transmission of the knowledge, ideas, and values that make up a given culture, from the ten commandments to this entry, is done through language. Again, language is an aspect from which humans differ to animals in degree rather than kind. Once more it is other large primate who share similarities with our species. Though these primates lack the larynx structure that allows for sophisticated vocalisation, there are other ways of communicating. The famous female gorilla, Koko, was taught to communicate in American sign language, and she taught it to other gorillas as well.

Culture does not mean civilization. It's not necessary to have cities in order to have a culture. Every society does the best it can with its circumstances. Any given social group, and therefore the culture that reflects it, is therefore neither more advanced nor more backward than any other; it is simply the way it is because that way works. If the circumstances should change due to environmental change, population pressure, or historical events, then the culture changes.

From an anthropological perspective, none are wrong, and none are right. There is therefore no 'white man's burden' to 'lift up' the so-called 'third world' countries. An agrarian society (such as Bali) shouldn't be forced into a capitalistic world that uses money simply because other countries see themselves as more advanced.

In the practical sense a culture norm is a society's propensity towards certain ideals; their aversion from others; and their standard, ritualistic practices. Essentially what the 'norm' is a summation of typical activities and beliefs of group of people.

"Culture norm" is essentially a gentle stereotype. Often times a culture norm is fairly obvious, for instance Anglo-America is primarily capitalist, monogamous, religious with emphasis in liberal education for youth. However, objections of course arise when other culture groups come out and object.

However, in some views the culture norm is a not a practical summation but a constant oppression. Certain religious sects' disdain for homosexuality is likely not viewed as a positive culture norm by homosexuals. But the tides have been turned, in the United States alone democracy, abolition and suffrage have triumphed over prior abhorrence.

One of the pioneers objecting to culture norms was Ayn Rand and her philosophy of Objectivism. In one of Rand's seminal works, The Fountainhead, she advances that the individual should have priorities over the society, as long as they do encroach on other individuals. This, opposite of altruistic practices like nationalism and patriotism, put the human ego as the ultimate judgment, not the culture. Thus, to her, it was not an act of rebellion but of right to disregard the thoughts of the masses for the self.

The culture norm stills exists, rampant in incessant public polling and ever-churning statistics. Essentially the picture present is not inaccurate per se, but everything is presented in dichotomies, disregarding middle ground and the gray areas that arise. Much of politics is approached and thus defined in polarization of this sort; this has seeped into (or came from) foreign policy, gaining cliché with George W. Bush's address to Congress in which a nation was "with us [the United States], or against us." The way one views other countries, cultures or regions, like at this time the Middle East, is very much defined by the 'gentle stereotype' of social norms, i e they are Islamic, their women are veiled, etc.

But, just as our approach to ourselves leaves out the finer points of our culture, this leaves out the finer points of cultures abroad. Still it cannot be said that culture norms are not a useful tool is assessing foreign entities, or ourselves.

MEME

A **meme** (pronounced like "beam") is an idea which spreads, sometimes described as a "contagious information pattern." In more specific terms, a meme is a self-propagating unit of cultural evolution, analogous to the gene (the unit of biological evolution). The term was coined by Richard Dawkins in his controversial book *The Selfish Gene*. The concept predates the coining of the term; for example, William S. Burroughs' assertion that "Language is a virus". Memes can represent parts of ideas, languages, tunes, designs, skills, moral and esthetic values and anything else that is commonly learned and passed on to others as a unit. The study of memes is called **memetics**.

In casual use, the term *meme* is sometimes used to mean any piece of information passed from one person to another. This is much closer to the analogy of "language as a virus" than it is to Dawkins's analogy of memes as replicating behaviours.

Overview

"The key to every man is his thought. Sturdy and defying though he look, he has a helm which he obeys, which is the idea after which all his facts are classified. He can only be reformed by showing him a new idea which commands his own."—Ralph Waldo Emerson

Dawkins observed that cultures can evolve in much the same way populations of organisms do, by passing ideas from one generation to the next, some of which may enhance or detract from the survival of the person holding them, thereby affecting which of those ideas continue to be passed on to future generations. For example, early cultures may have had different designs and methods for building tools. The culture with the more effective method may well have prospered while others suffered, leading to its method being adopted by a higher proportion of the population as time passed. Each tool design thus acts somewhat similarly to a biological gene; some populations have it and some don't, and the presence of the design in future generations is directly affected by the meme's function.

A key characteristic of a meme is that it is propagated by imitation. Whatever you learn by observing someone else doing it is potentially a meme. Observing is not limited to seeing (as in seeing how a tool is made); you can observe by hearing (a song or a story), smelling (an ingredient for a recipe), touching (a weapon to insure it's strong enough), or by reading. Because memes propagate by imitation from one individual to another, they could not exist without brains that are powerful enough to assess the key aspects of the behavior to be imitated (what to copy and why) as well as its potential benefits. Memes (or behaviors acquired and propagated by imitation) have been observed in just a few species on Earth, including humans, dolphins and a bird that learns how to sing by imitating its parents.

Both genes and memes can "live" much longer than the individual organisms that carry them. A successful gene (such as a gene for powerful teeth in a population of lions) can remain unchanged in the gene pool for tens/hundreds of thousands of years, and even more. A successful meme can propagate itself from one individual to another long after it has first appeared.

Unlike biological genes whose success is determined by how good at surviving the organism that carry them is, memes' success depends on more subtle means (such as criticism, persuasion, and fashion/peer pressure) that have not yet been widely investigated. A few common tricks that some of the most successful memes have been "using" to "propagate" themselves include:

1. "Find" an issue or a problem of interest which can not be solved (e.g. what, if anything, happens after

death) and "propose" a solution (e.g., you go to heaven or hell). The idea can't be proved wrong for sure, and as such is relatively safe and fit for further propagation.

2. "Frighten" those who would prefer not to propagate you (e.g. If you do, or do not do this, you will burn in hell) and "compensate" those who do as you "say" (e.g. Do this and you will go to heaven after you die).
3. "Ask" the individuals who carry you to be kind to other people and to spend a lot of time thinking and talking about you (e.g., a priest doing little else besides trying to spread his religion).

The quotes draw your attention to the fact that a meme does not purposely do or want anything—it just gets copied or not.

Examples of Memes

The following statements are crudely stated versions of some common memes:

"Statement X is true. Statement X tells us: If you believe X, you will go to heaven. If you do not believe X, you will go to hell. Therefore, it is your moral duty to convince everyone of the truth of X." (some skeptics believe this explains most organized religion: note that Statement X can be *anything*, so long as it contains this hook)

"I am a lucky person. Here are some stories of my luck. If you believe in good luck, you can become lucky like me." (and its obverse: see luck).

"You must send this message to five other people, or something bad will happen to you" (see chain letter)

All your base are belong to us

The concept of memes is itself a meme.

Evolution of Memes

Evolution requires not only inheritance and natural selection, but also mutation, and memes clearly have this property as well. Ideas that get passed on may undergo changes that accumulate over time. Folk tales and myths, for example, are often embellished in the retelling to make them more memorable—and therefore more likely to be retold again. More modern examples can be found in the various urban legends and hoaxes that circulate on the Internet, such as the Goodtimes virus warning.

Some of these methods of cultural evolution have been called "artificial selection", in contrast to "natural selection", to emphasize the fact that human choices are involved. But the distinction is not always clear: even evolution in nature involves conscious choices, and many choices we make may be influenced by our biology.

Biological Analogies

In much the same way that the selfish gene concept can be used as a point of view from which to better understand and reason about biological evolution, the meme concept can be used to better understand some otherwise puzzling aspects of human culture (and learned behaviors of other animals as well). However, if "better" is not good enough to test empirically, the question will remain whether the meme concept is good enough for science. Is the meme idea itself simply embedding itself in culture like other bad ideas?

A controversial application of this "selfish meme" parallel is the idea that certain collections of memes can act as "memetic viruses": collections of ideas that behave like independent life forms, and continue to get passed on even at the expense of their hosts simply because they are good at getting passed on. It has been suggested that evangelical religions behave this way; by including the act of passing on their beliefs as a moral virtue, other beliefs of the religion also get passed along even if they aren't particularly valuable to the believer.

Others note that the wide prevelance of human adoption of religious ideas proves that they *must* have some ecological, sexual, ethical or moral value. For example, most religions urge peace and cooperation among their followers ("Thou shalt not kill"), which may tend to promote the biological survival of social groups that carry these memes. Certainly religious promoters *claim* such value for following their rules or principles—but how is that related to what they feel is divine?

There is a tendency in memetics to disparage the religious meme. It is surprising to many memetics advocates to learn of meme-like concepts described long ago, which are prevalent in Sufi teaching. For an introduction to the *muwakkals,* the Eastern memes, read *The Music of Life,* Pir Hazrat Inayat Khan, Omega Uniform Edition, 2nd edition, 1993, trade paperback: 353 pages, ISBN 093087238X Muwakkals are considered separate beings, elementals, that make up human thought.

Memetics

Memetics is the formal study of memes. Memetics can currently be regarded as either a field of sociology, or a protoscience in its own right. Memetics applies concepts taken from the theory of evolution (especially population genetics) to human culture. It tries to explain many very controversial subjects, like religions and politica systems, using mathematical models.

Many thoughtful people wonder if the analogy of gene to culture will hold up and how the similarity would be tested. Memetics must be distinguished from sociobiology. In sociobiology the evolving entities are genes, while in memetics they are memes. Sociobiology is concerned with the biological basis of human behaviours, while memetics treats humans as products not only of biological evolution, but of cultural evolution also.

Memetic association is the discovery that memes herd. For example, the meme for bluejeans includes memes for trouser flies, riveted clothing, blue dye, cotton clothing, belt loops, and double-sewn seams.

Memetic drift is the process of an idea or meme changing as it is transferred from one person to another. Very few memes show strong **memetic inertia** which is the characteristic of a meme to be expressed in the same way and to have the same impact, regardless of which person is receiving or transmitting the idea. Memetic drift increases when the meme is transmitted by an awkward way of expressing the idea, whilst memetic inertia is strengthened when the form of expression rhymes or uses other mnemonic devices to preserve the memory of the meme prior to its transmittal. The article on Murphy's law shows one example of memetic drift.

Much of memetic terminology is created by prepending 'mem(e)-' to an existing, usually biological, term, or by putting 'mem(e)' in place of 'gen(e)' in various terms. Examples include: meme pool, memotype, memetic engineer, meme-complex.

CULTURE OF INDIA

The **culture of India** is one of the oldest cultures known to humanity.

Cultural policy

The cultural policy of the Government of India has three major objectives:

Preserving the cultural heritage of India, inculcating Indian art consciousness amongst Indians and promoting high standards in creative and performing arts.

History

The most endearing aspects of Indian art and architecture prior to colonization has been the strong impact of folk idioms and folk art on courtly art. Although folk art received little encouragement during the period of colonization, independence brought forward a renewed interest in folk paintings.

Traditions

Indians join their hands (palms together) and bow down in front of the other person, and say Namaste, Namaskar, or Pranam. This signifies reverent salutations.

Festivals in India are characterized by colour, gaiety, enthusiasm, prayers and rituals. Diwali, the popular festival of Indians, celebrates the return of Lord Rama and Sita from exile.

Indian Fashion

Indian fashion is rich in tradition, vibrant in colors and truly beautiful. Bold colors and metallics created by the inventive drapes of these textiles catches the imagination like no other contemporary clothing.

Indian dress designers combine Western trends with Indian touch, creating garments which are truly outstanding.

Drama and Theatre

Indian drama and theatre is perhaps as old as its music and dance. The tradition of folk theatre is alive in nearly all the linguistic regions of the country. In addition, there is a rich tradition of puppet theatre in rural India.

Dance

India offers a number of classical dance forms, each of which can be traced to different parts of the country. Each form represents the culture and ethos of a particular region or a group of people

There are many types of dance in India, from those which are deeply religious in content to those which are danced on more trivial happy occasions.

Painting

Indian painting is an old tradition, with ancient texts outlining theories of color and anecdotal accounts suggesting that it was common for households to paint their doorways or indoor rooms where guests resided.

Cave paintings from Ajanta, Bagh and Sittanvasal and temple paintings testify to a love of naturalism.

Recreation and sports

In the area of recreation and sports India had evolved a number of games. One would be surprised to know today that games like, Chess, Snakes and Ladders, Playing cards, Polo, the martial arts of Judo and Karate had originated as a sport in India and it was from here that these games were transmitted to foreign countries, where they were further modernized.

Festivals of India

Festivals in India are characterized by color, gaiety, enthusiasm, prayers and rituals. Foreign travelers are struck by the scale and multiplicity of Indian festivals that have evolved in the society.

Diwali, the popular festival of Indians, celebrates the return of Lord Rama and Sita from exile. Diwali is also called as the festival of lights. It usually falls between 15th October and 15th November. It is celebrated because on that day hundreds of years ago lord ram returned home to Ayodhya after 14 years of being into exile.

It also celebrates the day Mother Goddess destroyed a demon called 'Mahisha' & Victory of Good over evil. The day is celebrated by lighting lamps, diyas, visiting relatives, feasting, and displaying fireworks.

DIWALI—THE FESTIVAL OF LIGHTS

Links for Indian Festivals:

Diwali Festival in India, Diwali India, Diwali Pictures

Holi ecards.

Other Festivals in India

The word festival means feast day, festive celebration. As kids, when there used to be festivals the only thing that came to our minds was holidays and sweets that in turn meant lots of fun. India being a society of may religions there are a lot many festivals. For the Hindus there is diwali, for the Muslims there is id, for the Christians its Christmas and for the Parsis it's the New Year and apart from all these days there are two other days that are celebrated by all Indians irrespective of cast, creed or sex.

Yes, its 26th January and 15th August. i.e. republic day and the Independence Day.

Dusshera in India is another festival celebrated by the Hindus. It marks the victory of good over evil. On that day lord ram killed the evil Ravana. On dusshera an effigy of Ravana is burnt at many places.

Ramzan Id is the most important festival in the Muslim calendar. A month long fasting and prayers is followed by Ramzan Id. It's said that during this month all the prayers and wishes of an individual comes true.

Christmas in India—Christmas marks the birth of Jesus Christ on 25th December every year and is an inseparable part of Christians all over the country and the world. Santa Claus, gifts, cakes, cookies, and the beautifully decorated Christmas tree with a midnight mass depicts he beginning of Christmas.

Easter is another important festival for Christians. It's usually falls in the month of March or April. 40 days fast is followed by Good Friday and Easter. On this day Jesus Christ rose from the dead and ascended into heaven. Easter eggs and Easter bunnies are a major attraction during Easter.

Parsi New Year is one of the most important days in the Parsi community. It marks the beginning of a New Year filled with joy and prosperity.

15th august is celebrated by all Indians because on this day in the year 1947 India received independence from the British rule in India. Holi is another festival that is celebrated by all communities. It's a festival of colours. It marks the beginning of summer season and so water balloons are burst to beat the heat.

Some other festivals that are celebrated happily all over the country are Onam, Baisakhi, Pongal, Mahavir Jayanti, Buddha Jayanti, Guru Purnima, Raksha Bandhan, Krishna Janmashtami, Gandhi Jayanti, Kumbh Mela, Children's day, Ganesh Chaturthi and many many more festivals.

Festivals bring joy and happiness in our lives. If we celebrate all festivals alike we can spread the message of joy, happiness, brotherhood and humanity among one another and live as one family and community.

Indian Fashion

Indian Fashion - ancient fashion in India

Ancient Indian fashion garments generally used no stitching although Indians knew about sewing. Most clothes were ready to wear as soon as they left the loom. The traditional Indian Dhoti, the Scarf or Uttariya, and the popular Turban are still visible India and continue to be part of Indian fashion. Likewise, for women, the Dhoti or the Sari as the lower garments, combined with a Stanapatta forms the basic ensemble, and once again consists of garments that do not have to be stitched, the stanapatta being simply fastened in a knot at the back.

And the Dhoti or the Sari worn covering both legs at the same time or, in the alternative, with one end of it passed between the legs and tucked at the back in the fashion that is still prevalent in large area of India. Indian men and women for these garments in the usually hot Indian climate. - dhoti when he speaks of 'turbans used for trousers', and a kaupina when he is speaking of 'a rag of two fingers' breadth bound over the loins.

Indian sari remains the traditional clothing of Indian women. Worn in varied styles, it is a long piece of flat cotton, silk or other fabric woven in different textures with different patterns. The *sari* has a lasting charm since it is not cut or tailored for a particular size. This graceful feminine attire can also be worn in several ways and its manner of wearing as well as its color and texture are indicative of the status, age, occupation, region and religion of a woman. The tightly fitted, short blouse worn under a *sari* is called a *choli*. The *choli* evolved as a form of Indian clothing around the tenth century AD and the first *cholis* were only front covering; the back was always bare.

Another popular attire of women in Indian clothing is the *Indian salwar-kameez*. This popular Indian dress evolved as a comfortable and respectable garment for women in Kashmir and Punjab region, but is now immensely popular in all regions of India. *Salwars* are pyjama-like trousers drawn tightly in at the waist and the ankles. Over the *salwars*, women wear a long and loose tunic known as a *kameez*. One might occasionally come across women wearing a *churidar* instead of a salwar. A *churidar* is similar to the salwar but is tighter fitting at the hips, thighs and ankles. Over this, one might wear a collarless or mandarin-collar tunic called a *kurta*.

Though the majority of Indian women wear traditional Indian dresses, the men in India can be found in more conventional western clothing like shirts and trousers.

However, men in Indian villages are still more comfortable in traditional attire like *kurtas, lungis, dhotis* and pyjamas. Indian dresses & styles are marked by many variations, both religious and regional and one is likely to witness a plethora of colors, textures and styles in garments worn by the Indians.

Use of Gold in Indian Fashion: For this reason, some gold ornament is usually worn against the skin at all times.

Indian Gold ornaments are popular because the metal is believed to have the power purify anything it touches. Ornaments of gold and other metals, often combined with precious and semi-precious gems and beads, are popular with both men and women in India. Traditionally, Indian ornaments had economic significance for women too. The ornaments given to her at her wedding constituted a daughter's inheritance from her father (Dowry). Customarily land and other property was divided among the sons; though this no longer holds true. In addition, a bride's ornaments were financial security throughout her life.

Ornaments of Indian Fashion

Nose pin: More common than a nose ring, both are symbols of purity & marriage, though today many unmarried Indian girls wear this adornment.

Necklace: These are very popular fashion accessories across India amongst girls and women of all ages. Necklaces are made of a variety of materials, ranging from glass beads to gold and diamonds. One special necklace is the mangalasutra, worn only by married Indian women. It is the Indian equivalent of the western wedding ring. Traditionally a woman wore it during her wedding ceremony and took it off only if her husband died.

Bangles: Worn on the wrist, bangles are believed to be protective bands and women always wore them as symbolic guards over their husbands. As with other ornaments, bangles today are worn by women of all ages all over India and are made of silver, gold, wood, glass, and plastic, among other materials.

Ear rings: Rings, studs and other ornaments worn in the ears are popular all over the country. In fact, a girl's ears are usually pierced before her first birthday.

Other important ornaments are finger rings, toe rings and anklets. Rings for the fingers are again, of various materials and designs and worn by unmarried and married women. Since the ring has become a common adornment, it is no longer considered a symbol in Indian marriages.

However, toe rings and anklets are still worn mostly by married women. Ornaments for the feet are usually made of silver because gold, being a 'pure' metal, was not supposed to be worn on the feet. This privilege was given only to women of royal Indian families. In addition to these ornaments is the 'mangatika' or 'tikli'. This ornament, worn at the top of the forehead in the parting of the hair, is usually a small pendant on the end of a chain that is clasped to the hair. Although traditionally this ornament was also worn as a symbol of marriage, today it is not so commonly worn even by married women.

Kajal or Eyeliner : From the time a child is six days old, its mother applies kajal to its eyes and also a small black dot on the forehead to mar the child's beauty. This 'imperfection' is said to protect from evil.

Sindoor : dot on forehead of woman indicating married status of Indian Women, power, protection for her husband. It is applied by the husband as part of wedding ceremony.

Indian Drama

Indian drama and theatre is perhaps as old as its music and dance. Classical theatre traditions have also influenced modern theatre, particularly the Hindi, Marathi and Bengali theatres. The tradition of folk theatre is alive in nearly all the linguistic regions of the country. In addition, there is a rich tradition of puppet theatre in rural India.

The Sangeet Natak Akademi located in Delhi has performed the role of sponsoring, research, dissemination, appreciation and patronage of the performing arts. It gives awards to outstanding performers and provides assistance for theatre production and teaching and offers scholarships to students and exchange of troupes.

The National School of Drama also located in Delhi teaches stage direction, acting and related subjects. It also has a Repertory Company of its own.

Indian art is also an art of social, political and religious influences. It changed and evolved with the evolution of a civilization which was full of remarkable innovations in all areas of artistic expression. The cultural policy of the Government of India has three major objectives - preserving the cultural heritage of India, inculcating Indian art consciousness amongst Indians and promoting high standards in creative and performing arts.

Western scholars have often had difficulty understanding the complex cultural and philosophical systems that gave birth to Indian art tradition. The story of Indian art is also the story of the oldest and the most resilient culture on earth. It is seen as an amalgamation of indigenous and outside influences, yet having a unique character and distinctiveness of its own.

Indian art features spirals and curvaceous lines, vines and tendrils, round-figured goddesses, circular amulets, colored gemstones, arches and domes, haloed deities, crescent moons, and the globe of the sun. Indian sculptures and paintings depict the diversity, colour and spontaneity of this country and are representations of the all-encompassing nature of Indian culture.

The story of Indian art is also the story of the oldest and the most resilient culture on earth. It is seen as an amalgamation of indigenous and outside influences, yet having a unique character and distinctiveness of its own. Indian art is also an art of social, political and religious influences. It changed and evolved with the evolution of a civilization which was full of remarkable innovations in all areas of artistic expression. Indian art features spirals and curvaceous lines, vines and tendrils, round-figured goddesses, circular amulets, colored gemstones, arches and domes, haloed deities, crescent-moons, and the globe of the sun. Indian sculptures and paintings depict the diversity, colour and spontaneity of this country and are representations of the all-encompassing nature of Indian culture.

The most endearing aspects of Indian art and architecture prior to colonization has been the strong impact of folk idioms and folk art on courtly art. Although folk art received little encouragement during the period of colonization, independence brought forward a renewed interest in folk paintings.

Indian Paintings

Indian paintings traditions go back to antiquity, as is evident from the murals of Ajanta, Ellora and other frescoes, the Buddhist palm leaf manuscripts, the Jain texts and the Deccan, Mughal and Kangra schools of miniature Indian painting.

Indian Painting is an old tradition, with ancient texts outlining theories of color and and anecdotal accounts suggesting that it was common for households to paint their doorways or indoor rooms where guests resided. Cave paintings from Ajanta, Bagh and Sittanvasal and temple paintings testify to a love of naturalism.

Indian paintings provide an aesthetic continuum that extends from the early civilization to the present day. This form of art in India is vivid and lively, refined and sophisticated and bold and vigorous at the same time. From being essentially religious in purpose in the beginning, Indian paintings have evolved over the years to become a fusion of various traditions which influenced them.

At first glance, an Indian miniature painting, to the uninitiated, appears nothing more than a clutter and tangle of pastoral settings, dominated by masculine and feminine figures. Yet these scenes are not detached visions of artistic expression but provide the basis of Indian music and art forms.

Most of these masterly works are visual creations of emotional and perceptive concepts that depict the *ragas* or musical modes of Indian classical music. Miniature painters employed at various medieval courts, discovered the potential of limitless self-expression in their depiction and today there are 130 known sets of such miniatures.The Indian paintings have now acquired a stature of their own. They use materials and techniques from all over the world but express Indian realities and Indian experiences.

The respect for tradition and the ability to transcend it at the same time is clearly evident in Indian art of today. This is the essence of what has been described as the eclecticism of the Indian contemporary expression.

Starting with the Bengal school, many contemporary painters have been influenced by modern styles.

Indian Dances illuminate & express India's culture in a direct manner, playing on the sensibilities of the onlooker.

India offers a number of classical dance forms, each of which can be traced to different parts of the country. Each form represents the culture and ethos of a particular region or a group of people

There are many types of dance in India, from those which are deeply religious in content to those which are danced on more trivial happy occasions.

Classical Indian Dances are usually always spiritual in content, although this is often true also of Folk dances. The most popular classical styles seen on the Indian dance stage are Bharatanatyam of Tamil Nadu, Kathakali and Mohiniyattam of Kerala, Odissi of Orissa, Kathak of Uttar Pradesh, Kuchipudi of Andhra Pradesh and Manipuri of Manipur

Indian mythology, legends and classical literature provide the themes of the Indian dance, both of the classical and folk variety. The classical dance is based on rigid rules and dance discipline. Its forms include Bharat Natyam, Kuchipudi, Oddissi and Kathak as also a tradition of dance-dramas-Kathakali, Kutiyattam, Mohiniattam, etc.

Indian dance is divided into nritta - the rhythmic elements, nritya - the combination of rhythm with expression and natya-the dramatic element.

Nritya is usually expressed through the eyes, hands and facial movements. Nritya combined with nritta makes up the usual dance programmes.

Sports in India : The history of sports in India dates back to the Vedic era. Physical culture in ancient India was fed by a powerful fuel--religious rites. There were some well-defined values like the mantra in the Atharva-Veda, saying," Duty is in my right hand and the fruits of victory in my left". In terms of an ideal, these words hold the same sentiments as the traditional Olympic oath: ".......For the Honour of my Country and the Glory of Sport."

Badminton probably originated in India as a grownup's version of a very old children's game known in England as battledore and shuttlecock, the battledore being a paddle and the shuttlecock a small feathered cork, now usually balled a "bird."

In the area of recreation and sports India had evolved a number of games. One would be surprised to know today that games like, Chess, Snakes and Ladders, Playing Cards, Polo, the martial arts of Judo and Karate had originated as a sport in India and it was from here that these games were transmitted to foreign countries, where they were further modernized.

It is more than likely that many of today's Olympic disciplines are sophisticated versions of the games of strength and speed that flourished in ancient India and Greece. Chess, wrestling, polo, archery and hockey (possibly a fall-out from polo) are some of the games believed to have originated in India.

Hockey, in which India has an impressive record with eight Olympic gold medals, is officially the national sport. Other popular games are football, cricket, basketball, volleyball and badminton. Cricket has become a very popular game in India. After the IX Asian Games in New Delhi in 1982, the capital city now has modern sports facilities. Such facilities are also being developed in other parts of the country. Besides sports and games included in the international sporting agenda, there are many which have developed indigenously. Among these are wrestling and several traditional systems of martial arts.

Deviant behavior is a *behavior* that is not accepted in the society or organizations. *Crime* is a good instance of this, but other behaviors caused by cultural difference can be seen as deviance. *Formal* and *informal social controls* attempt to prevent and minimize deviance, both serious deviance such as *murder* and trivial deviance such as *picking* *one's nose.* It also means not doing what the majority does or alternatively doing what the majority does not do. It doesn't necessarily mean criminal behavior.

In *classical economics* and all *micro-economics* **labour** is one of three *factors of production,* the others being *land* and *capital.* It is a measure of the work done by human beings. There are macro-economic system theories which have created a concept called *human capital,* although counterposing macro-economic system theories that think human capital is a contradiction that mixes apples with oranges.

Compensation and Measurement

The price of labour is called a **wage**, and the price of labour per period of time is referred to as the **wage rate**.

In Labor Economics, the following terms are defined:

wage = payment per unit of time (typically an hour)

earnings = payment per over a period (typically a week, a month, or a year)

total compensation = earnings + benefits

income = total compensation + *unearned income*

economics rent = total compensation - *opportunity cost*

Economists measure labour in terms of hours worked, total wages, or *efficiency.*

Job

In general, the word **job** refers to any discrete activity of economic production. In this sense, a group may divide up a set of tasks among its members, each task being "the job" of the individual it is assigned to.

However, in *capitalist* societies, the word "job" has become synonymous with "*employment*". This refers to the long term relationship between a labourer and those who have legal control of the other factors of production. In this sense, labourers talk of "getting a job", or "having a job".

This *conceptual metaphor* of a "job" as a possession has led to its use in slogans such as "money for jobs, not bombs". Similar conceptions are that of "land" as a possession (*real estate*) or *intellectual rights* as a possession (*intellectual property*).

None of the three are recognized in traditional *labour economics* which emphasizes work, not entitlements or even necessarily royalties, as the basis of rights to receive economic benefits.

Kinds of labour: brain worker, free-work, manual labour, slavery, telework, volunteer

SOCIAL ROLE

In *sociology*, a **role** or **social role** is a set of connected *behaviours*, as conceptualised by *actors* in a social *situation*. It is mostly defined as an expected *behaviour* in a given *individual social status*. The spelling **rôle** is also used.

The *term* is used in two rather different but related *senses*. It is vital to both *functionalist* and *interactionist* understandings of *society*, but is of only peripheral *relevance* to *conflict theory*.

Role confusion is a *situation* where an *individual* has *trouble* determining which role he/she should play. For example, you, a *college student*, go to attend an *convention* of *fun club* and find your *teacher* there. Should you behave as a *student* or as an *enthusiast* who shares the same *interest*?

Role strain characterises a situation where fulfilling a certain role has a *conflict* with fulfilling another role. For example, you found your teacher made a *mistake* and should you report that? If you did, you might disgrace him and if you didn't, you might not fulfil your role as student. While role conflict takes place across different *role sets*, role strain happens within the same role set.

Role in Functionalist and Consensus Theory

The functionalist *approach*, which is largely borrowed from *anthropology*, sees a "role" as the set of *expectations* that *society* places on an *individual*. By unspoken *consensus*, certain *behaviours* are deemed "appropriate" and others "inappropriate". For example, it is appropriate for a *doctor* to dress fairly conservatively, ask a series of personal *questions* about one's *health*, touch one in ways that would normally be forbidden, write *prescriptions*, and show more *concern* for the personal *wellbeing* of his *clients* than is expected of, say, an *electrician* or a *shopkeeper*.

Notice that "role" is what the doctor *does* (or, at least, is expected to do), while *status* is what the doctor *is*. In other words, "status" is the *position* an *actor* occupies, while "role" is the expected behaviour attached to that position. Roles are not limited to occupational status, of course, nor does the fact that one is cast in the role of "doctor" during working hours prevent one from taking other on other roles at other times: *husband*, golf club, *president*, *father*, and so on.

Roles can be semi-permanent ("doctor", "mother", "child"), or transitory. A well-known example is the *sick role* as formulated by *Talcott Parsons* in the late *1940s*. A person who is judged to be "sick" is exempted from his usual roles; is not held personally *responsible* for his *incapacity*; can only take on the *sick role* on condition that he wants to eventually get well and return to a "normal" role; and he must co-operate with his officially designated *helpers* (doctors and others).

Role conflict takes place when one is forced to take on two different and incompatible roles at the same time. Consider the example of a *doctor* who is himself a *patient*, or who must decide whether he should be present for his daughter's *birthday party* (in his role as "father") or attend an ailing patient (as "doctor"). (Also compare the *psychological* concept of *cognitive dissonance*.)

In the functionalist *conception*, role is one of the important ways in which individual *activity* is socially regulated: roles create regular *patterns* of *behaviour* and thus a *measure* of *predictability*, which not only allows individuals to function effectively because they know what to expect of others, but also makes it possible for the *sociologist* to make *generalisations* about *society*. Collectively, a *group* of interlocking roles creates a *social institution*: the *institution* of *law*, for example, can be seen as the *combination* of many roles, including "*police officer*", "*judge*", "*criminal*", and "*victim*".

Roles, in this conception, are created by society as a whole, are relatively inflexible, are more-or-less universally agreed upon, and individuals simply take their designated roles on and attempt to fulfil them as best they can. Although it is recognised that different roles interact ("teacher" and "student"), and that roles are usually defined in relation to other roles ("*doctor*" and "*patient*", or "*mother*" and "*child*") , the functionalist approach has great *difficulty* in accounting for *variability* and *flexibility* of roles, and finds it difficult to account for the vast *differences* in the way that individuals conceive different roles. Taken to extremes, the functionalist approach results in "role" becoming a set of static, semiglobal *expectations* laid down by a unified, amorphous society: as simply *prescriptions* for *correct behaviour*. The *distinction* between "role" and *norm* and *culture* thus becomes sterile.

Nevertheless, although the classic *functionalist* approach to "role" is no longer regarded as an especially useful *tool* in the modern sociologist's approach to understanding societies, it remains a fundamental concept which is still taught in most introductory *courses* and is still regarded as important, particularly so when considering relatively homogenous, united societies like the middle-class post-war *USA* that gave *birth* to it.

More broadly, "role" in this static, defined-by-the-whole-of-society *sense*, is a *concept* that has crossed over from *academic discourse* into popular use. It has become *commonplace* to speak of particular "roles" as if they were indeed fixed, agreed on by all, and uncontroversial: "the role of the teacher" or "a parent's role", for example. Notice that this everyday usage nearly always employs "role" in a normative way, to imply that "this is the *proper* behaviour" for a teacher or a parent, or even for an entire *institution* such as the *government.*

Role in Interactionist or Social Action Theory

In *interactionist* social theory, the concept of role is crucial. The interactionist *definition* of "role" pre-dates the *functionalist* one (which is a later borrowing from the same source), but is more fluid and subtle, and remains a more fruitful concept. Oddly enough for a concept which has been adopted by two of the three major *branches* of *sociology* and is central to a good deal of *anthropology* as well, the first systematic use of the term "role" was made by a *philosopher*, *George Herbert Mead,* in his seminal 1934 work, *Mind, self and society.*

A role, in this conception, is not fixed or prescribed but something that is constantly negotiated between individuals in a tentative, *creative* way. Mead's main interest was the way in which *children* learn how to become a part of society by imaginative *role-taking*. Children, wrote Mead, imitate the roles of the *people* around them and try them on to see how well they fit. This is always done in an interactive way: it's not meaningful to think of a role for one person alone, only for that *person* as an *individual* who is both co-operating and competing with others. *Adults* behave similarly: taking roles from those that they see around them, adapting them in creative ways, and (by the process of social *interaction*) testing them and either confirming them or modifying them. This can be most easily seen in encounters where there is considerable *ambiguity*, but is nevertheless something that is part of all social interactions: each individual actively tries to "define the situation" (understand her role within it); choose a role that is advantageous or appealing; play that role; and persuade others to support the role.

MODERNITY

Modernity is a type, mode, or stage of *society*, initially confined to the recent history of *West European* countries from the *Renaissance* to the rise of *mass media*, and characterized by a larger-scale integration of formerly isolated *local communities* and departure from tradition and religion toward *individualism*, rational or scientific organization of society, and *egalitarianism*. A society in the state of modernity is called a modern society. The process of a society becoming a modern society is called *modernization*. The most defining events in the modern period include:

Rise of the *nation state*,

Industrialization,

Rise of *capitalism*,

Emergence of *socialist countries*,

Rise of *representative democracy*,

Increasing role of *science* and *technology*,

Urbanization,

Proliferation of *mass media*,

The more particular events in the West European history include:

The *Age of Discovery*

The *Renaissance*

The Enlightenment

The Reformation and *Counter Reformation*

The *French Revolution*

The *American Revolution*

The *Industrial Revolution*

It is usually suggested that some or most of these events led to the more complete realization of modern society in Europe.

Defining Characteristics of Modernity

There have been numerous attempts, particularly in the field of *sociology*, to understand what modernity is. A wide variety of terms are used to describe the society, social life, driving force, symptomatic mentality, or some other defining aspects of modernity.

They include: *Bureaucracy*, *Disenchantment of the world*, *Rationalization*, *Secularization*, *Alienation*, *Commodification*, *Decontexutalization*, *Individualism*, *Subjectivism*, *Linear-progression*, *Objectivism*, *Universalism*, *Reductionism*, *Chaos*, *Mass society*, *Industrial society*, Homogenization, Unification, Hybridization, Diversification, *Democratization*, Centralization, Hierarchical organization, Mechanization, *Totalitarian*, and so on.

Modernity is often characterized by comparing modern societies to *premodern* or *postmodern* ones, and the understanding of those non-modern social statuses is, again, far from a settled issue. To an extent, it is reasonable to doubt the very possibility of a descriptive concept that can adequately capture diverse realities of societies of various historical contexts, especially non-European ones, let alone a three-stage model of social evolution from premodernity to postmodernity.

However, in terms of social structure, many of the defining events and characteristics listed above stem from a transition from relatively isolated local communities to a more integrated large-scale society. Understood this way, modernization might be a general, abstract process which can be found in many different parts of histories, rather than a unique event in Europe.

In general, large-scale integration involves:

Increased movement of goods, *capital*, people, and information among formerly separate areas, and increased influence that reaches beyond a local area.

Increased formalization of those mobile elements, development of 'circuits' on which those elements and influences travel, and standardization of many aspects of the society in general that is conducive to the mobility.

Increased specialization of different segments of society, such as the *division of labor*, and interdependency among areas. Seemingly contradictory characteristics ascribed to modernity are often different aspects of this process. For example, unique *local culture* is invaded and lost by the increased mobility of cultural elements, such as recipes, folktales, and hit songs, resulting in a cultural homogenization across localities, but the repertoire of available recipes and songs increases within a area because of the increased interlocal movement, resulting in a diversification within each locality. (This is manifest especially in large *metropolises* where there are many mobile elements).

Centralized bureaucracy and hierarchical organization of governments and firms grows in scale and power in an unprecedented manner, leading some to lament the stifling, cold, rationalist or totalitarian nature of modern society. Yet individuals, often as replaceable components, may be able to move in those social subsystems, creating a sense of liberty, dynamic competition and individualism for others. This is especially the case when a modern society is compared with premodern societies, in which the *family* and *social class* one is born into shapes one's lifecourse to a greater extent.

These social changes are somewhat common to many different levels of social integration, and not limited to what happened to the West European societies in a specific time period. For example, these changes might happen when formerly separate virtual communities merge. Similarly, when two human beings develop a close relationship, communication, convention, and increased division of roles tend to emerge.

Another example can be found in ongoing globalization-the increased international flows changing the landscape for many. In other words, while modernity has been characterized in many seemingly contradictory ways, many of those characterizations can be reduced to a relatively simple set of concepts of social change.

At the same time, however, such an understanding of modernity is certainly not satisfactory to many, because it fails to explain the global influence of West European and American societies since the Renaissance. Mere large-scale integration of local communities, seen in the *Macedonia* of *Alexander the Great* or the *Mongolia* of the *Khans*, would not necessarily result in the same magnitude of influence as the West European modernization. What has made Western Europe so special?

There have been two major answers to this question. First, an internal factor is that only in Europe, through the Renaissance humanists and early modern philosophers and scientists, rational thinking came to replace many intellectual activities that had been under heavy influence of convention, superstition, and *religion*. This line of answer is most frequently associated with *Max Weber*, a sociologist who is known to have pursued the answer to the above question.

Second, an external factor is that *colonization*, starting as early as the *Age of Discovery*, created exploitative relations between European countries and their colonies. This view has notably been explored by the world systems theory of *Emanuel Wallerstein*.

It is also notable that such commonly-observed features of many modern societies as the *nuclear family*, *slavery*, *gender roles*, and nation states do not necessarily fit well with the idea of rational social organization in which components such as people are treated equally. While many of these features have been dissolving, histories seem to suggest those features may not be mere exceptions to the essential characteristics of modernization, but necessary parts of it.

Modernity as Hope, Modernity as Doom

Modernization brought a series of seemingly undisputable benefits to people. Lower *infant mortality rate*, decreased death from *starvation*, eradication of some of the fatal diseases, more equal treatment of people with different backgrounds and incomes, and so on. To some, this is an indication of the potential of modernity, perhaps yet to be fully realized. In general, rational, scientific approach to problems and the pursuit of economic wealth seems still to many a reasonable way of understanding good social development.

At the same time, there are a number of dark sides of modernity pointed out by sociologists and others.

Technological development occurred not only in the medical and agricultural fields, but also in the military. The *atomic bombs* dropped on *Hiroshima* and *Nagasaki* during *World War II*, and the following *nuclear arms race* in the post-war era, are considered by some as symbols of the danger of technologies that humans may or may not be able to handle wisely.

Stalin's Great Purges and the *Holocaust (or Shoah)* are considered by some as indications that rational thinking and rational organization of a society might involve exclusion, or extermination, of non-standard elements. It is pointed out by some that homosexuals, criminals, and the mentally ill are also among the excluded in the modern society.

Environmental problems comprise another category in the dark side of modernity. *Pollution* is perhaps the least controversial of these, but one may include decreasing *biodiversity* and *climate change* as results of development. The development of *biotechnology* and *genetic engineering* are creating what some consider sources of unknown risks.

Besides these obvious incidents, many critics point out psychological and moral hazards of modern life - alienation, feeling of rootlessness, loss of strong bonds and common values, *hedonism*, and so on. This is often accompanied by a re-evaluation of pre-modern communities, though such criticism may slip into a nostalgia for an idealized past.

CHARACTERISTICS OF SOCIOLOGICAL WRITING

What are the most important things to keep in mind as you write in sociology? Pay special attention to the following issues:

Argument

The first thing to remember in writing a sociological argument is to be as clear as possible in stating your thesis. Of course, that is true in all papers, but there are a couple of pitfalls common to sociology that you should be aware of and avoid at all cost. As previously defined, sociology is the study of the interaction between individuals and larger social forces. Different traditions within sociology tend to favor one side of the equation over the other, with some focusing on the agency of individual actors and others on structural factors. The danger is that you may go too far in either of these directions and thus lose the complexity of sociological thinking. Although this mistake can manifest itself in any number of ways, three types of flawed arguments are particularly common: the "individual argument," the "human nature argument," and the "society argument."

The "individual argument" generally takes this form: "The individual is free to make choices, and any outcomes can be explained exclusively through the study of his or her ideas and decisions." While it is of course true that we all make our own choices, we must also keep in mind that, to paraphrase Marx, we make these choices under circumstances given to us by the structures of society. Therefore, it is important to investigate what conditions made these choices possible in the first place, as well as what allows some individuals to successfully act on their choices while others cannot.

The "human nature argument" seeks to explain social behavior through a quasi-biological argument about humans, and often takes a form such as: "Humans are by nature X, therefore it is not surprising that Y." While sociologists disagree over whether a universal human nature even exists, they all agree that it is not an acceptable basis of explanation. Instead, sociology demands that you question why we call some behavior natural, and to look into the social factors which have constructed this "natural" state.

The "society argument" often arises in response to critiques of the above styles of argumentation, and tends to appear in a form such as: "Society made me do it." Students often think that this is a good sociological argument, since it uses society as the basis for explanation. However, the problem is that the use of the broad concept "society" masks the real workings of the situation, making it next to impossible to build a strong case.

This is an example of reification, which is when we turn processes into things. Society is really a process, made up of ongoing interactions at multiple levels of size and complexity, and to turn it into a monolithic thing is to lose all that complexity. People make decisions and choices. Some groups and individuals benefit, while others do not. Identifying these intermediate levels is the basis of sociological analysis.

Although, each of these three arguments seems quite different, they all share one common feature: they assume exactly what they need to be explaining. They are excellent starting points, but lousy conclusions.

Evidence

Once you have developed a working argument, you will next need to find evidence to support your claim. What counts as evidence in a sociology paper? First and foremost, sociology is an empirical discipline. Empiricism in sociology means basing your conclusions on evidence that is documented and collected with as much rigor as possible. This evidence usually draws upon observed patterns and information from collected cases and experiences, not just from isolated, anecdotal reports. Just because your second cousin was able to climb the ladder from poverty to the executive boardroom does not prove that the American class system is open.

You will need more systematic evidence to make your claim convincing. Above all else, remember that your opinion alone is not sufficient support for a sociological argument. Even if you are making a theoretical argument, you must be able to point to documented instances of social phenomena that fit your argument. Logic is necessary for making the argument, but is not sufficient support by itself.

Sociological evidence falls into two main groups: quantitative and qualitative.

Quantitative data are based on surveys, censuses, and statistics. These provide large numbers of data points, which is particularly useful for studying large-scale social processes, such as income inequality, population changes, changes in social attitudes, etc.

Qualitative data, on the other hand, comes from participant observation, in-depth interviews, data and texts, as well as from the researcher's own impressions and reactions. Qualitative research gives insight into the way people actively construct and find meaning in their world.

Quantitative data produces a *measurement* of subjects' characteristics and behavior, while qualitative research generates information on their *meanings* and practices. Thus, the methods you choose will reflect the type of evidence most appropriate to the questions you ask. If you wanted to look at the importance of race in an organization, a quantitative study might use information on the percentage of different races in the organization, what positions they hold, as well as survey results on people's attitudes on race. This would measure the distribution of race and racial beliefs in the organization. A qualitative study would go about this differently, perhaps hanging around the office studying people's interactions, or doing in-depth interviews with some of the subjects. The qualitative researcher would see how people act out their beliefs, and how these beliefs interact with the beliefs of others as well as the constraints of the organization.

Unfortunately, much of sociology has split into two armed camps over methodological questions. Many tend to exclusively favor qualitative over quantitative data, or vice versa, and it is perfectly reasonable to rely on only one method in your own work. However, since each method has its own strengths and weaknesses, combining methods can be a particularly effective way to bolster your argument. Do not be too quick to limit yourself to only one approach.

These distinctions are not just important if you have to collect your own data for your paper. You also need to be aware of them even when you are relying on secondary sources for your research. In order to critically evaluate the research and data you are reading, you should have a good understanding of the strengths and weaknesses of the different methods.

Units of Analysis

Given that social life is so complex, you need to have a point of entry into studying this world. In sociological jargon, you need a unit of analysis. The unit of analysis is exactly that: it is the unit that you have chosen to analyze in your study. Again, this is only a question of emphasis and focus, and not of precedence and importance. You will find a variety of units of analysis in sociological writing, ranging from the individual up to groups or organizations. You should choose yours based on the interests and theoretical assumptions driving your research. The unit of analysis will determine much of what will qualify as relevant evidence in your work. Thus you must not only clearly identify that unit, but also consistently use it throughout your paper.

Let's look at an example to see just how changing the units of analysis will change the face of research. What if you wanted to study globalization? That's a big topic, so you will need to focus your attention. Where would you start?

You might focus on *individual human actors,* studying the way that people are affected by the globalizing world. This approach could possibly include a study of Asian sweatshop workers' experiences, or perhaps how consumers' decisions shape the overall system.

Or you might choose to focus on *social structures or organizations.* This approach might involve looking at the decisions being made at the national or international level, such as the free-trade agreements that change the relationships between governments and corporations. Or you might look into the *organizational structures of corporations* and measure how they are changing under globalization. Another structural approach would be to focus on the *social networks* linking subjects together. That could lead you to look at how migrants rely on social contacts to make their way to other countries, as well as to help them find work upon their arrival.

Finally, you might want to focus on *cultural objects or social artifacts* as your unit of analysis. One fine example would be to look at the production of those tennis shoes the kids seem to like so much. You could look at either the material production of the shoe (tracing it from its sweatshop origins to its arrival on the showroom floor of malls across America) or its cultural production (attempting to understand how advertising and celebrities have turned such shoes into necessities and cultural icons).

Whichever unit of analysis you choose, be careful not to commit the dreaded *ecological fallacy*. An ecological fallacy is when you assume that something that you learned about the group level of analysis also applies to the individuals that make up that group. So, to continue the globalization example, if you were to compare its effects on the poorest 20% and the richest 20% of countries, you would need to be careful not to apply your results to the poorest and richest individuals.

These are just general examples of how sociological study of a single topic can vary. Because you can approach a subject from several different perspectives, it is important to decide early how you plan to focus your analysis and then stick with that perspective throughout your paper. Avoid mixing units of analysis without strong justification. Different units of analysis generally demand different kinds of evidence for building your argument. You can reconcile the varying levels of analysis, but doing so may require a complex, sophisticated theory, no small feat within the confines of a short paper. Check with your instructor if you are concerned about this happening in your paper

TYPICAL WRITING ASSIGNMENTS IN SOCIOLOGY

So how does all of this apply to an actual writing assignment? Undergraduate writing assignments in sociology may take a number of forms, but they typically involve reviewing sociological literature on a subject; applying or testing a particular concept, theory, or perspective; or producing a small-scale research report, which usually involves a synthesis of both the literature review and application/test.

The Critical Review

The review involves investigating the research that has been done on a particular topic and then summarizing *and evaluating* what you have found. The important task in this kind of assignment is to organize your material clearly and synthesize it for your reader. A good review does not just summarize the literature, but looks for patterns and connections in the literature and discusses the strengths and weaknesses of what others have written on your topic. You want to help your reader see how the information you have gathered fits together, what information can be most trusted (and why), what implications you can derive from it, and what further research may need to be done to fill in gaps.

Doing so requires considerable thought and organization on your part, as well as thinking of yourself as an expert on the topic. You need to assume that, even though you are new to the material, you can judge the merits of the arguments you have read and offer an informed .pinion of which evidence is strongest and why.

APPLICATION OR TESTING OF A THEORY OR CONCEPT

The application assignment asks you to apply a concept or theoretical perspective to a specific example. In other words, it tests your practical understanding of theories and ideas by asking you to explain how well they apply to actual social phenomena. In order to successfully apply a theory to a new case, you must include the following steps:

1. First you need to *have a very clear understanding of the theory itself*: not only *what* the theorist argues, but also *why* he or she argues that point, and how he or she justifies it. That is, you have to understand how the world works according to this theory and how one thing leads to another.
2. Next you should *choose an appropriate case study*. This is a crucial step, one that can make or break your paper. If you choose a case that is too similar to the one used in constructing the theory in the first place, then your paper will be uninteresting as an application, since it will not give you the opportunity to show off your theoretical brilliance. On the other hand, do not choose a case that is so far out in left field that the applicability is only superficial and trivial. In some ways theory application is like making an analogy. The last thing you want is a weak analogy, or one that is so obvious that it does not give any added insight. Instead, you will want to choose a happy medium, one that is not obvious but that allows you to give a developed analysis of the case using the theory you chose.
3. This leads to the last point, which is the *analysis*. A strong analysis will go beyond the surface and explore the processes at work, both in the theory and

> in the case you have chosen. Just like making an analogy, you are arguing that these two things (the theory and the example) are similar. Be specific and detailed in telling the reader how they are similar. In the course of looking for similarities, however, you are likely to find points at which the theory does not seem to be a good fit. Do not sweep this discovery under the rug, since the differences can be just as important as the similarities, supplying insight into both the applicability of the theory and the uniqueness of the case you are using.

You may also be asked to *test* a theory. Whereas the application paper assumes that the theory you are using is true, the testing paper does not makes this assumption, but rather asks you to try out the theory to determine whether it works. Here you need to think about what initial conditions inform the theory and what sort of hypothesis or prediction the theory would make based on those conditions. This is another way of saying that you need to determine which cases the theory could be applied to (see above) and what sort of evidence would be needed to either confirm or disconfirm the theory's hypothesis. In many ways, this is similar to the application paper, with added emphasis on the veracity of the theory being used.

Research Paper

Finally, we reach the mighty research paper. Although the thought of doing a research paper can be intimidating, it is actually little more than the combination of many of the parts of the papers we have already discussed. You will begin with a critical review of the literature and use this review as a basis for forming your research question. The question will often take the form of an application ("These ideas will help us to explain Z.") or of hypothesis testing ("If these ideas are correct, we should find X when we investigate Y."). The skills you have already used in writing the other types of papers will help you immensely as you write your research papers.

And so we reach the end of this all-too-brief glimpse into the world of sociological writing. Sociologists can be an idiosyncratic bunch, so paper guidelines and expectations will no doubt vary from class to class, from instructor to instructor. However, these basic guidelines will go a long way to help you get started.

GROUP (SOCIOLOGY)

In *sociology*, a **group** is usually defined as a collection of *humans* or *animals*, who share certain characteristics, interact with one another, accept expectations and obligations as members of the group, and share a common *identity*. Using this definition, *society* can appear as a large group.

While an *aggregate* comprises merely a number of individuals, a group in sociology exhibits cohesiveness to a larger degree. Characteristics that members in the group may share include *interests*, *values*, ethnic/linguistic background, and *kinship* ties.

Types of Groups

Primary groups consist of small groups with intimate, kin-based relationships: families, for example. They commonly last for years. The term was coined by *Charles Horton Cooley*. They are small and display face to face interaction.

Secondary groups, in contrast to primary groups, are large groups whose relationships are *formal* and *institutional.* Some of them may last for years but some may disband after a short lifetime. The formation of primary groups happens within secondary groups.

Individuals almost universally have a bond toward what *Muzafer Sherif* called "**Reference Groups**". These are groups to which the individual does not have real membership, but to which he conceptually relates him/herself, and from which he might accept goals and values as a part of his/her self identity.

Common use vs Precise Definition

The dictionary gives an origin of 1686 and an *etymological* meaning of "lump" or "mass". A general definition is "an assemblage of objects standing near together, and forming a collective unity; a knot (of people), a cluster(of things)". There were also special definitions for art, music, and mathematics.The dictionary quotation by the famous British editor and author Walter Bagehot (1826-1877) offers an important and traditional perspective on the necessity of understanding groups: "Man can only make progress in cooperative groups."

Muzafer Sherif (1916-1982) was a founder of the discipline of *social psychology*. He introduced innovative techniques in to the research on all of the factors that go into making up a group during the period of 1940s and 1970s. His most famous study of 11 and 12 yr old boys with his wife Carolyn, and other colleagues and students is known as the Robber's Cave Study. He formulated a more technical definition with the following elements:

A social unit consisting of a number of individuals interacting with each other with respect to:

1. Common motives and goals;

2. An accepted division of labor, i.e. roles,
3. Established status (social rank, dominance) relationships;
4. Accepted norms and values with reference to matters relevant to the group;
5. Development of accepted sanctions (praise and punishment) if and when norms were respected or violated.

This definition is long and complex, but it is also precise. It succeeds at providing the researcher with the tools required to answer three important questions:

1. "How is a group formed?";
2. "How does a group function?";
3. "How does one describe those social interactions that occur on the way to forming a group?"

But this article will not elaborate on the tradition of Sherif. Rather, it will focus on the description of those social behaviors of individuals that do not qualify as groups under the Sherif definition or on the same behaviors that are displayed when a group fails to form, malfunctions, or disperses.

Significance of the Definition

The attention of those who use, participate in, or study groups has been focused on adequately functioning groups, with larger organizations, or with the decisions made in these organizations. Much less attention has been paid to the more ubiquitous and universal social behaviors that do not clearly demonstrate one or more of the five necessary elements described by Sherif.

Perhaps the earliest efforts to understand these social units has been the extensive descriptions of urban street gangs in the 1920s and 1930s, continuing through the 1950s, which understood them to be largely reactions to the established authority. The primary goal of gang members was to defend gang territory, and to define and maintain the dominance structure within the gang. There remains in the popular media and urban law enforcement agencies an avid interest in gangs, reflected in daily headlines which emphasize the criminal aspects of gang behavior. However, these studies and the continued interest have not improved the capacity to influence gang behavior or to reduce gang related violence.

The relevant literatures on animal social behaviors, such as work on territory and dominance, have been available since the 1950s. However, they have been largely neglected by policy makers, sociologists and anthropologists. Indeed, vast literatures on organization, property, law enforcement, ownership, religion, warfare, values, conflict resolution, authority, rights, and families have grown and evolved without any reference to any analogous social behaviors in animals. This disconnect may be the result of the belief that social behavior in humankind is radically different from the social behavior in animals because of the human capacity for language use and rationality. And of course, while this is true, it is equally likely that the study of the social (group) behaviors of other animals might shed light on the evolutionary roots of social behavior in humans.

Territorial and dominance behaviors in humans are so universal and commonplace that they are simply taken for granted (though sometimes admired, as in home ownership, or deplored, as in violence). But these social behaviors and interactions between human individuals play a special role in the study of groups: *they are necessarily prior to the formation of groups*. The psychological internalization of territorial and dominance experiences in conscious and unconscious memory are established through the formation of *personal identity*, body concept, or *self concept*. An adequately functioning individual identity is necessary before an individual can function in a division of labor (role), and hence, within a cohesive group. Coming to understand territorial and dominance behaviors may thus help to clarify the development, functioning, and productivity of groups.

Development of a Group

If one brings a small collection of strangers together in a restricted space and environment, provide a common goal, and maybe a few ground rules, a predictable flow of behavior will follow. Interaction between individuals is the basic requirement. At first, individuals will differentially interact in sets of twos or threes while seeking to interact with those with whom they share something in common: i.e., interests, skills, and cultural background. Relationships will develop some stability in these small sets, in that individuals may temporarily change from one set to another, but will return to the same pairs or trios rather consistently and resist change. Particular twosomes and threesomes will stake out their special spots within the overall space.

Again depending on the common goal, eventually there will be integration of twosomes and threesomes into larger sets of six or eight, and corresponding revisions of territory, dominance ranking, and further differentiation of roles. All of this seldom takes place without some conflict or disagreement: for example, fighting over the distribution of resources, the choices of means and different subgoals, the development of what are appropriate norms, rewards and punishments. Some of these conflicts will be territorial in nature: i.e., jealousy over roles, or locations, or favored relationships. But most will be involved with struggles for status, ranging from mild protests to serious verbal conflicts and even dangerous violence.

By analogy to animal behavior, these behaviors can be termed *territorial behaviors* and *dominance behaviors*. Depending on the pressure of the common goal and on the various skills of individuals, differentiations of leadership, dominance, or authority will develop. Once these relationships solidify, with their defined roles, norms, and sanctions, a productive group will have been established.[5,6,7]

Aggression is the mark of unsettled dominance order. Productive group cooperation requires that both dominance order and territorial arrangements (identity, self concept) be settled with respect to the common goal and with respect to the particular group. Often some individuals will withdraw from interaction or be excluded from the developing group. Depending on the number of individuals in the original collection of strangers, and the number of hangers-on that are tolerated, one or more competing groups of ten or less may be formed, and the competition for territory and dominance will then also be manifested in the intergroup transactions.

Dispersal and Transformation of Groups

Two or more people in interacting situations will over time develop stable territorial relationships. As described above, these may or may not develop into groups. But stable groups can also break up in to several sets of territorial relationships. There are numerous reasons for stable groups to malfunction or to disperse, but essentially this is because of loss of compliance with one or more elements of the definition of group provided by Sherif. The two most common causes of a malfunctioning group are the addition of too many individuals, and the failure of the leader to enforce a common purpose, though malfunctions may occur due to a failure of any of the other elements (i.e., confusions status or of norms).

In a society, there is obvious need for more people to participate in cooperative endeavors than can be accommodated by a few separate groups. The military has been the best example as to how this is done in its hierarchical array of squads, platoons, companies, battalions, regiments, and divisions. Private companies, corporations, government agencies, clubs, and so on have all developed comparable (if less formal and standardized) systems when the number of members or employees exceeds the number that can be accommodated in an effective group. Not all larger social structures require the cohesion that may be found in the small group. Consider the neighborhood, country club, or the megachurch, which are basically territorial organizations who support large social purposes. Any such large organizations may need only islands of cohesive leadership.

For a functioning group to attempt to add new members in a casual way is a certain prescription for failure, loss of efficiency, or disorganization. The number of functioning members in a group can be reasonably flexible between five and ten, and a long-standing cohesive group may be able to tolerate a few hangers on. The key concept is that the value and success of a group is obtained by each member maintaining a distinct, functioning identity in the minds of each of the members. The cognitive limit to this *span of attention* in individuals is often set at seven. Rapid shifting of attention can push the limit to about ten. After ten, subgroups will inevitably start to form with the attendant loss of purpose, dominance order, and individuality, with confusion of roles and rules. The standard classroom with twenty to forty pupils and one teacher is a rueful example of one supposed leader juggling a number of subgroups.

Weakening of the common purpose once a group is well established can be attributed to: adding new members; unsettled conflicts of identities (i.e., territorial problems in individuals); weakening of a settled dominance order; and weakening or failure of the leader to tend to the group. The actual loss of a leader is frequently fatal to a group, unless there was lengthy preparation for the transition. The loss of the leader tends to dissolve all dominance relationships, as well as weakening dedication to common purpose, differentiation of roles, and maintenance of norms. The most common symptoms of a troubled group are loss of efficiency, diminished participation, or weakening of purpose, as well as an increase in verbal aggression. Often, if a strong common purpose is still present, a simple reorganization with a new leader and a few new members will be sufficient to re-establish the group, which is somewhat easier than forming an entirely new group.

TERRITORY AND DOMINANCE

History

There were no concepts of territory and dominance to inform the theory of Sociology in its formative stages. Great bodies of literature have developed on social relations, family, property, law enforcement, aggression, and others with only slight mention of territory or dominance. It was not until the 1950s that scientists in human psychology, human socialization, and animal social behavior began to meet together to try to integrate their perspectives. But the professional disciplines' traditions, basic concepts, and research methodologies were difficult to reconcile. Psychoanalysis, with its focus on introspection, and subjective data, had become the accepted theory for many psychologists and sociologists. However, the Macy Foundation did sponsor five annual scientific conferences, and published the proceedings in five volumes entitled *Group Processes* between 1954 and 1958.

Territory and Dominance are basic, primitive, and well studied social behaviors in many animals, including humans and other primates. These two well-differentiated categories of social behavior can be considered as evolutionary and developmental twins in that they are profoundly connected. It's difficult to make observations about one without commenting on the other. Yet, they are clearly differentiated. Obviously, for example, territories can be invaded, captured, or destroyed by more dominant individuals. But an individual occupying his/her own territory does have an advantage in the struggle for possession of that territory, and is able to exert increased strengths when defending his own.

Recognition of Territorial Behavior

Territory was initially identified as a physical space which may be staked out by individuals singly or as mating pairs. The space is subsequently defended, sometimes quite vigorously, and when left by the owner there is the strong tendency to return to it. Territories may also be claimed by various aggregates of individuals such as families, tribes, or nations. Each species has well defined patterns of when, and how territory is defined and defended. Nesting behavior in birds, hunting territory in wolves, or home ownership in humans are easy phenomena to identify. However, this initial definition was elaborated to include not only other human objects such as friends, spouses, children, but domestic animals, pets of all kinds, and physical objects such as toys, jewelry, automobiles , and golf clubs.

Territories are strongly defended. When they are lost, sold, stolen or captured, there may be in humans an intense sense of loss, very much akin to depression. Animals also have analogous reactions, but are naturally devoid of the expressions of emotion in language. Territory is functionally related to the survival behaviors of seeking food, shelter, sex, and reproduction, but there is no effort here to establish the survival value of territory or dominance. The universal presence of these principles in a wide variety of species would seem to argue for *survival value*, but there is, as yet, no scientific methodology to establish either validity or falsification of survival value.

Over the long period of evolutionary time, humankind has developed a most complicated array of territorial behaviors that range from personal social relationships, to possession of land, property, and physical objects. Through the intermediation of spoken and written language, territory can be extended to abstract and symbolic objects and ideas such as religion, school, value systems, and jobs. The most obvious human territorial behaviors are the establishment of a home base, and home ownership. This extends to the ownership of many objects considered as property such as furniture, car, clothes, golf clubs, and so on. The use of the possessive pronouns (mine, yours, his, hers, ours, theirs) is a valid signal of territorial behavior recognized in self and others.

Dominance behavior was first scientifically identified as the pecking order in chickens. But, of course, authority, differences in strength, intellect, and social rank in humans have been identified in literature and history as far back as there are records. The simplest marker for dominance is that one individual can do something to another that cannot be done in return. Aggression and fighting are markers of the absence of an established dominance order. Peaceful coexistence is the marker of the existence of a stable dominance order. Human beings have creatively defined, rationalized, and institutionalized many markers of dominance and authority, ranging from uniforms, titles, insignia of rank, to tone of language, mode of address, the corner office suite, size of bank account, make of car, and so on, to the next new word, symbol, or innovative marker.

Family Territory and Dominance

The family is an available, familiar, and informative social structure to use as an exemplar of the interactions of territory and dominance. This section will explore some of the ways that families exhibit territory and dominance behaviors. For the purpose of exposition, it will leave aside an unresolved variety of opinions about some of the issues discussed, i.e., revised definitions of the family.

In heterosexual nuclear families, there is usually a preexisting bond and history of interaction (courtship or dating) between a man and a woman before a family is considered formed. Other research in social psychology has provided information on the great variations in the mating selection process; however, none of these variations contradict the basic necessity of a bonding interaction between a man and a woman for the purpose of species maintenance. Most often there is an implied intention to reproduce.

Indeed, sexual intercourse is a specific, required type of interaction for reproduction which undoubtedly can contribute strength of purpose to the pair's bond. Additional strength is usually contributed by the lengthy pregnancy and birth of a child. This is not to deny that pair territorial bonds may be weakened, or disrupted by other factors before, during, and after the pregnancy and delivery. The birth of a baby creates the strongest of territorial bonds—the mother-child relationship -- and is famous for affecting (for good or bad) the husband-wife bond.

The birth of the child into a family is a clear and uncontroverted example that many of the early and stronger territorial bonds of an individual are provided without personal selection or choice by the individual. The child immediately acquires many potential territories: a mother and a father, often siblings and other relatives, an important spacial relationship to the arms of the mother, perhaps the breast of the mother, a blanket, and a cuddle toy, and a geographical home.

Likewise over time the child involuntarily acquires numerous attitudes: to life, religion, social relationships, sex, aggression, learning, and so on through the complicated life from zero to six years of age. Gradually the child has some choice and preference in the selection of some objects, such as toys, and some types of food. There are, of course, examples of some young babies rejecting their nurses. Whatever the theoretical and technical flaws of Freudian psychoanalysis and psychotherapy, the thousands of hours of observation and verbalizations by subjects in these procedures provides innumerable examples of the importance of these involuntary, but long durational territorial relationships, as well as the conflicts between them.

History, biography, and fiction provides the public with multiple examples of the variations in patterns over time, culture, and even next door neighbors. But the basic patterns of family territorial bonding remain unchallenged, including homosexual families with or without formal marriage. Body (self) image, and personal identity are two of the most important dynamic territories derived over the early and late interactions and territorial bonding that occur within the family structure.

Dominance relationships within marriage and family are as familiar and as inevitable as the territorial relationships. Aristotle described the man as being the master and manager of his household to include wife, children, slaves, the ox and plough, and property. Roman law specified this to include the power of life and death over children. This is no longer the accepted pattern today, but not even the most unobservant can deny the existence of a dominance order within every family. Many of the subtleties of territorial or dominance behavior may be taken as "just the way things are" or "the kids always fight".

Dominance patterns are universal, but not rigidly determined. Learning, culture, circumstances, as well as individual intentional efforts are continuously molding the patterns. Many women may be the overall dominant individual in the family. Some men may be subordinate in earning income, but take the leading child care role. Most modern families will have a unique pattern of shared responsibilities and dominance, but some form of dominance is inevitable, or the family would be totally dysfunctional. The rule that a stable dominance order is required for a properly functioning group is equally pertinent to the family. Most families do not function as groups, and they are not considered as such, despite the suggestion of such in the introduction to this article.

Likewise, it is perhaps the rare family that doesn't manifest some conflict within it: conflict between the mother and father and assorted relatives; sibling conflict; conflict between children and parents; conflict over money and distribution of time and other resources; and adolescents are famous for their rebelliousness. Most conflict is over who can do what to whom, or who has what kind of access to some resource or privilege. Conflict does not necessarily weaken territorial bonds, even though some conflicts last for years, or forever.

Every social worker who has responsibility for children is well aware that an abused child will often vigorously resist being removed from an abusing mother, and will return to the mother if allowed. The same territorial principle helps to explain why some abused wives return again and again to an abusive husband.

Intensity, Modification, and Change of a Territory

Human territorial bonds are formed by the dynamic interaction of individuals with objects whether other individuals, physical objects, abstract ideas, religions, schools, or football teams. Territorial bonds vary in intensity and duration depending on the frequency of interaction, the intensity of the interaction, and the duration of the interaction.

It is unlikely that a child with a reasonable normal childhood will ever forget his or her mother, but the territorial child/ mother bond can be attenuated by separation in adulthood, by infrequency of face to face interaction, failures to visit or communicate, and so on. But most people remain alert to their maternal bonding for their lifetimes. Similarly the mating and marriage bond can undergo severe dilution by divorces, deaths, and remarriages, and lack of interaction. But it is the rare man or woman who can not cite chapter and verse about a series of marriages, or intense relationships if motivated to do so. It is important to realize that there is nothing imperative about territory.

The tendency to act in a territorial manner is deeply inborn in humans, but it is also quite modifiable by culture, learning, custom, habit, time, and most of all by replacement territories. The average individual has weak territorial feelings, and a few active memories about primary school, stronger ones about high school, even stronger about college, and perhaps still stronger about professional schools such as law, and medicine.

The latter schools' territorial bonding may be somewhat weaker as the individual transfers much of the territorial bonding to the profession that he or she actually practices, and interacts with on a daily basis. The territorial feeling about the practice of law or medicine can be quite strong and the territory vigorously defended. But one does not have to be a member of a profession to have a territorial bond to one's job. Many people from mechanics to secretaries and wallpaper hangers take pride in their jobs and their job skills. Others are simply dependent on their jobs for their livelihood, and are frightened by any threat to their wellbeing or survival whatever the cause.

Organization

Another clearly defined function of territoriality and dominance is portrayed as the span of supervision and authority, as well as the normal flow of decision making and implementation up and down the tables of organization for all types of organizations, military, religious, or corporate with special reference to decisions under the designations of authority and identification. Perhaps it is not too late to consider territory and dominance as the unifying concepts that the early sociologists searched for so avidly and unsuccessfully in their comparative studies of different societies from primitive to the most complex.

SOCIOLOGY OF CHILDHOOD

History

In the last two or three decades the sociology of childhood has gained increasing attention and triggered numerous empirical studies as well as intensive theoretical disputes, starting in the Scandinavian and the English-speaking countries. Up to this time, sociology had approached children and childhood mainly from a socialization perspective, and the emergence of the new childhood sociological paradigm ran parallel to the feminist critique of sociological traditions. Childhood sociologists attacked the "adultocentric" approach and the "separative view" of sociology towards children. Not surprisingly, then, the key works in the sociology of childhood are quite interdisciplinary, linking *history*, *cultural studies*, *ethnomethodology*, and *pedagogy*.

Recent Trends

The current Sociology of childhood is organised around two central discussions:

The Child as a Social Actor

This approach derives from youth sociology as well as ethnography. Focussing on everyday life and the ways children orientate themselves in society, it engages with the cultural performances and the social worlds they construct and take part in. Theory and research methodology approach children as active participants and members of society right from the beginning. Thus they are neither analyzed as outsiders to society nor as merely 'emergent' members of society. Therefore, the sociology of childhood distinguishes itself from the established concepts of *socialization* research and *developmental psychology* of the last decades.

The Generational Order

The second approach centres on socio-structural and socio-theoretical questions concerning *social equality* and *social order* in a society, which categorizes their members by age and segregates them in many respects (rights, deeds, economical participation, ascribed needs etc.). These issues can be summarized under the overall concept of the "*generational order*".

Thus, the categorization of societal members by age is far from being an innocent representation of natural distinctions, but rather a social construction of such a "natural truth". It is, therefore, a relevant component of *social order* and deeply connected to other dimensions of social inequality. Social and economic changes and socio-political interventions thus become central topics in childhood sociology. The analysis of these issues has increased awareness of the generational inequality of societies.

CURRENT TASKS

Questions about socialization practices and institutions remain central in childhood research. But, they are being dealt with in a new, more sociological way. To analyze socialization processes means, therefore, to reconstruct the historically and culturally varying conceptions, processes and institutions of *disciplining* and *civilisation* of the offspring. In addition, the strategies of *habitus* formation and the practices of *status* (re-)production are considered. The *sociology of social inequality* and the *sociology of the family* and private life are, therefore, important fields for childhood sociologists.

Children's own action, their resistance, cooperation, and collective action among *peers* has to be taken into account.

Meanwhile widespread anthropological assumptions concerning a universal human nature , based on a view of individual and society as opposed to each other, should be omitted from the conceptual repertoire of sociological childhood research. They are the legacy of the older socialization approach and they legitimate some forms of childhood and education practices as indispensable and even as a "natural" requirement of society, while devaluing others. In this way they generally legitimate western middle class childhood and mask social inequality and the interests of social order.

❑❑❑